Outdoor
Fun and
Games
for kids

hamlyn

Outdoor Fun and Games for kids

Over 100 activities
for 3–11 year olds

Jane Kemp and Clare Walters

First published in Great Britain in 2007 by Hamlyn,
a division of Octopus Publishing Group Ltd
2–4 Heron Quays, London E14 4JP

Distributed in the United States and Canada by
Sterling Publishing Co., Inc.
387 Park Avenue South, New York, NY 10016–8810

ISBN-13: 978-0-600-61661-0
ISBN-10: 0-600-61661-4

A CIP catalogue record for this book is available from the British Library

Printed and bound in Dubai

10 9 8 7 6 5 4 3 2 1

Contents

Introduction

Welcome to the great outdoors! Playing games outside is a wonderful – and inexpensive – way for children and parents to enjoy themselves together. And, of course, regular periods in the fresh air are vital for children's well-being. The exercise involved in a lively game not only enables young muscles to grow strong, but also frequently helps to improve balance, coordination, dexterity and even concentration. And where children are playing with others, it also improves social skills.

In this book there are games for all ages up to and including 11 years, both alone or in a group. If you don't have enough children to play a favourite group game, it is usually easy to adapt it for just an adult and child (many of the games require an adult helper anyway, either to act as leader or referee, or to help prepare the props or set up the game). Under-fives especially are not too bothered about sticking to set rules – they're simply interested in having a good time with you.

How to use this book

The very youngest children will love the action games in Chapter 1, where popular rhymes are combined with movement and dancing. In some games, these actions are done in unison; in others, an individual child leads the play. In all cases the games are easy to learn and fun to sing together. And singing and dancing in a group is a great way to encourage early social skills, helping

young children to learn the essential arts of joining in, following others, waiting for their turn and cooperating together.

Outdoor games you can share with a single child in your own garden or backyard enable you to have fun at home, whether your child is alone or playing with other little friends. From simple obstacle courses to exciting treasure hunts, Chapter 2 has plenty of suggestions for ways to enjoy being outside in smaller spaces with a young child.

As children get older, hopping and skipping games become very popular, especially in the playground. In Chapter 3, you'll find simple hopping games, games for beginner skippers and games for more seasoned experts. These sorts of activities are not only very energetic, but also require a high level of skill and social interaction.

Most of us will remember playing 'He' or 'It' at school. And Chapter 4 is packed with other favourite run-and-chase games, from 'Stuck in the mud' to 'Follow my leader', to play in big spaces outside. These games are ideal for chilly winter days when everyone needs to keep active and run around to stay warm. They will bring a glow to the cheeks!

Ball games are popular with both boys and girls and span a wide age range, from first rolling activities suitable for little ones to more complex games with rules. The games in Chapter 5 will help to improve both hand–eye coordination and memory, as they involve throwing and catching, aiming, batting and remembering sequences. And, of course, they are very lively.

The team games in Chapter 6 are great for older children, and help to prepare them for the more formal sports they will encounter in secondary school, such as basketball or hockey. These games not only aid in developing an understanding of rules and strategies, but also teach children about working as a team. In addition they refine social skills, as children learn to become that most difficult of things – a good loser!

Long, hot summer holidays are likely to involve a spell at the beach, and this offers a whole new set of opportunities for outdoor games and activities. In Chapter 7 you'll find lots of fun things to do on the seashore, from hosting a sandcastle competition to playing beach cricket.

Finally, in Chapter 8, there are activities to help your child discover the natural world. If children learn to appreciate their surroundings early on, they will deepen their understanding of – and respect for – the environment we all share.

We do hope you and your children enjoy this selection of games to play outside. Have fun!

Skip to my Lou

Age range 4+
Number of players Several pairs plus one extra child
Energy level 2
What you will need No props

If you want a group of children to learn to mix together or overcome shyness, try this game, which involves children constantly changing their partners. The aim is to 'Skip to my Lou' until everyone in the ring has had a chance to dance with someone new.

How to play

Players form a circle, and one child stands in the middle of the ring while the others choose partners. An adult helper can make a pair if necessary. During the first verse the player in the ring chooses someone's partner and takes her to dance around the outside of the circle. Then they both rejoin the circle.

Variation

Another popular version of this song has these verses:

Flies in the buttermilk,
Shoo, shoo, shoo,
Flies in the buttermilk,
Shoo, shoo, shoo,
Flies in the buttermilk,
Shoo, shoo, shoo,
Skip to my Lou, my darlin'.

Cows in the cornfield,
What'll I do?
Cows in the cornfield,
What'll I do?
Cows in the cornfield,
What'll I do?
Skip to my Lou, my darlin'.

Lou, Lou, skip to my Lou,
Lou, Lou, skip to my Lou,
Lou, Lou, skip to my Lou,
Skip to my Lou, my darlin'.

Now the person who has lost his partner skips alone around the outside of the circle while the second verse is sung by all the children.

During the third verse he chooses a new partner from the circle and dances round the outside of the circle with her. Then they both rejoin the circle. And so the game goes on, with the new singleton in the middle and starting again at the first verse of the rhyme.

Lost my partner, what shall I do?
Lost my partner, what shall I do?
Lost my partner, what shall I do?
 Skip to my Lou, my darlin'.

Find another one, just like you,
Find another one, just like you,
Find another one, just like you,
 Skip to my Lou, my darlin'.

Ring-a-ring o' roses

Age range 3+
Number of players Two or more
Energy level 2
What you will need No props

This is one of the first – and most popular – dancing rhymes that children ever learn, resulting in everyone falling down in a happy heap at the end of the verse! Even the youngest child will enjoy it with a bit of adult help.

How to play
Hold hands in a circle – or facing each other, if there are only two of you. Then sing the rhyme below and follow the actions.

Ring-a-ring o' roses
(children walk round in a circle)

A pocket full of posies.
(children continue walking round in a circle)

A-tishoo, a-tishoo,
(children stand still and pretend to sneeze)

We all fall down!
(children fall down)

Variation
Try this verse for getting up again:

The cows are in the meadow
(children pat the floor)

Eating all the grass.
(children continue patting the floor)

A-tishoo, a-tishoo,
(children sit still and pretend to sneeze)

Who's up last!
(children all jump up)

Tip for beginners
Remind little ones to fall down gently – you don't want any bumped heads!

I sent a letter to my love

Age range 4+
Number of players Several
Energy level 1
What you will need An empty envelope

This is a sedate game for most of the time – but has a mad rush at the end of each verse when two children race each other for a single place in the circle. The aim is to keep your place if you receive the letter.

How to play

All the children sit in a circle apart from one. That one has the envelope – the 'letter' – and skips round the outside of the ring, dropping it behind one child as he gets to the end of the rhyme.

The child behind whom the letter has been dropped must now pick it up and, running in the opposite direction, race the first child round the outside of the circle to get back to his empty place and sit down again. If the first child beats him to it, then the other child gets to be the letter-bearer next time.

I sent a letter to my love
And on the way I dropped it.
One of you has picked it up
And put it in your pocket.
It wasn't you,
It wasn't you,
It wasn't you,
It was YOU!

Variation
You can still play this game if you only have two children playing – simply mark out the missing players' spaces with pebbles or two crossed sticks around the playing circle. Young children may enjoy using dolls or soft toys as stand-ins, too.

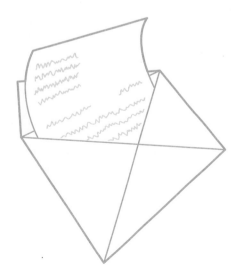

Gathering nuts in May

Age range 5+
Number of players Several pairs
Energy level 2
What you will need No props

This is a popular party game that can become rather boisterous, but is still fun to play outside with a smaller group of children. Players are trying to win someone over to their team from the opposing side in a tug-of-war.

How to play

Sing the rhyme below to the tune of 'Here we go round the mulberry bush' and follow the actions described. To begin, have two lines of children facing each other, a little distance apart.

1st verse: Both lines of children move towards each other, and then back again.

Here we go gathering nuts in May,
Nuts in May,
Nuts in May.
Here we go gathering nuts in May,
On a cold and frosty morning.

2nd verse: The first line moves towards and back from the second line, which remains still.

Who will you have for nuts in May?
Nuts in May,
Nuts in May.
Who will you have for nuts in May?
On a cold and frosty morning.

3rd verse: The second line chooses a child from the first line to name. Then it moves towards and back from the first line, which remains still.

We'll have [name of child] for nuts in May,
Nuts in May,
Nuts in May.
We'll have [name of child] for nuts in May,
On a cold and frosty morning.

4th verse: The first line moves towards and back from the second line, which remains still.

Who will you send to take her away?
Take her away,
Take her away.
Who will you send to take her away?
On a cold and frosty morning.

5th verse: The second line chooses a child from their side to name. Then it moves towards and back from the first line, which stays still.

We'll send [name of child] to take her away.
Take her away,
Take her away.
We'll send [name of child] to take her away.
On a cold and frosty morning.

The two named children then stand in the centre between the two lines and try to pull each other across to their own side, until one finally wins and joins the other's line. Then the game begins all over again with the opposite side choosing the names for the tug-of-war.

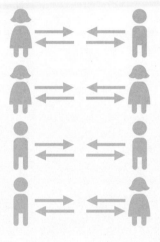

Verse one

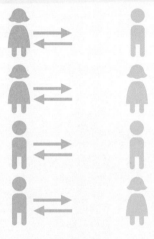

Verses two and four

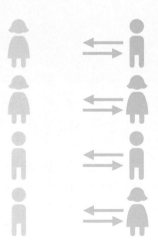

Verses three and five

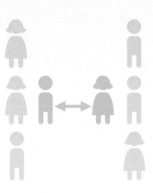

End

There was a princess long ago

Age range 4+
Number of players Eight or more in a circle; one or more with miming
Energy level 1
What you will need No props

If you are playing this game with just one child, simply mime the actions together, pretending to hold the reins for the handsome prince riding by – and dance holding hands together at the end.

How to play

Three children are chosen to be the princess, the fairy and the prince. The other children stand in a circle, with the princess in the middle, and chant or sing the first verse while walking round her.

There was a princess long ago,
Long ago, long ago.
There was a princess long ago,
Far, far away.

And she lived in a tall high tower...
(everyone raises their arms in an arch to make a tower)

One day a fairy waved her wand...
(the chosen fairy goes into the circle and waves a wand)

The princess slept for 100 years...
(the princess lies down and pretends to sleep, the others put their heads on their hands)

A great big forest grew around...
(everyone waves raised arms to form trees)

A handsome prince came riding by...
(the chosen prince skips round the circle)

He waved his sword and cut it down...
(the prince gently chops down a 'tree')

He took her hand and woke her up...
(the prince takes the princess's hand and she rises)

So everybody's happy now...
(everyone skips round the circle clapping their hands)

The farmer's in his den

Age range 3+
Number of players 12 or more
Energy level 2
What you will need No props

This is another favourite game with very young children, and is sometimes known as 'The farmer's in the dell'. The aim is to choose all the members of the farmer's family one by one.

How to play

Choose a 'farmer' to stand in the middle of a circle. Holding hands, the children walk round him singing the song. At the end of the first verse, they stand still while the farmer chooses a 'wife' to join him in the centre.

After each subsequent verse the last person to join the group chooses the next person, until there are six children in the centre: the farmer, his wife, her child, his nurse, her dog, his 'bone'. When the final verse is being sung everyone stands still and claps, except the bone. The next time the game is played, the bone becomes the farmer and a new set of children is chosen.

The farmer's in his den.
The farmer's in his den.
E-ie, e-ie, e-ie,
The farmer's in his den.

The farmer wants a wife.
The farmer wants a wife.
E-ie, e-ie, e-ie,
The farmer wants a wife.

The wife wants a child.
The wife wants a child.
E-ie, e-ie, e-ie,
The wife wants a child.

The child wants a nurse.
The child wants a nurse.
E-ie, e-ie, e-ie,
The child wants a nurse.

The nurse wants a dog.
The nurse wants a dog.
E-ie, e-ie, e-ie,
The nurse wants a dog.

The dog wants a bone.
The dog wants a bone.
E-ie, e-ie, e-ie,
The dog wants a bone.

We all clap the bone.
We all clap the bone.
E-ie, e-ie, e-ie,
We all clap the bone.

Variation

You can also play this game in the traditional way, where everyone pats the bone lightly, but this often gets too vigorous and you may end up with a rather tearful 'bone', so clapping is usually preferable.

In and out the dusty bluebells

Age range 4+
Number of players A large group of children
Energy level 2
What you will need No props

This starts in a fairly sensible fashion – but ends up with a line of giggly children struggling under a single arch! They are trying to make as long a line as possible weaving through the 'bluebells'.

How to play

The children form a circle holding hands, with their arms raised, and one child is chosen to be the leader. The game then proceeds as follows:

1st verse: The leader weaves in and out of the circle – the 'bluebells' – while everyone sings the song. On reaching the word 'partner', the leader goes to stand behind whichever child she has naturally stopped at.

In and out the dusty bluebells,
In and out the dusty bluebells,
In and out the dusty bluebells,
Who shall be my partner?

2nd verse: The leader now puts her arms on the shoulders of the child she is standing behind and gently taps him while singing the second verse.

Tippy, tippy, tappy on your shoulder,
Tippy, tippy, tappy on your shoulder,
Tippy, tippy, tappy on your shoulder,
You shall be my partner.

At the end of this verse the tapped child comes out of the circle, stands behind the leader and puts his arms on her shoulder. Now the first verse is sung again and the two children weave through the bluebells together in a line of two.

As the game goes on and the verses are repeated, the line gets longer and longer, until there is only one arch left – at which point the two children making the arch choose a child to 'capture' and he or she becomes the new leader.

Altogether now!

Age range 3+
Number of players One or more
Energy level 3
What you will need No props

Another first copying game that you can adapt to make as short or long as you like, depending on the time available. Players copy the various actions that are mentioned in the song.

Tip for beginners
If the children find it hard to stand on one leg, try easier actions, such as wiggling fingers, flapping elbows or nodding heads.

How to play
Sing or chant the song and do the actions, which are chosen either by an adult or by a different child each time. Add as many different actions as you want – the ones below are just suggestions. End the game by coming back to the first verse once more.

We all clap hands together,
We all clap hands together,
We all clap hands together,
As children like to do.

We all shake one leg together...

We all shake the other leg together...

We all touch our toes together...

We all run around together...

We all turn around the tree together...

We all bounce down together...

We all jump up together...

We all clap hands together!

Punchinello

Age range 3+
Number of players Two or more
Energy level 2
What you will need No props

This game can be played either with one child and a parent or with a group of children, who are trying to copy the actions of the player who has been chosen as Punchinello.

How to play

If you are a parent playing with your child on his own, stand him a little way off from you and ask him to walk/skip towards you while you chant the first verse.

If you have a group of children, choose one to be Punchinello. Punchinello then goes into the middle of the circle and skips one way round, while the other children walk in the opposite direction singing the rhyme.

At the end of the second verse, Punchinello must choose an action to do (see box, right). Then, throughout the third verse, the other person/children must copy him.

When the third verse is finished, the other person/another child becomes Punchinello, and the game begins again.

Who comes here? Punchinello, little fellow.
Who comes here? Punchinello, little man.

What can you do, Punchinello, little fellow?
What can you do, Punchinello, little man?

I'll/We'll do it too, Punchinello, little fellow,
I'll/We'll do it too, Punchinello, little man!

Actions to try

If a child doesn't know what actions to do, suggest some of these:
* Star jumps
* Hopping
* Stretching arms apart and then back into the chest
* Turning around and touching the ground
* Touching the toes
* Touching the opposite toe and hand
* Putting hands on hips and bending from side to side
* Flapping the arms
* Running on the spot
* Rubbing the tummy while tapping the head (very hard!).

Brown girl in the ring

Age range 4+
Number of players Two or more
Energy level 2
What you will need No props

This well-known Caribbean dancing rhyme probably originated in Jamaica. The game provides a great opportunity for children to show off their dancing skills to one another.

How to play

This is another game that you can play with just two of you, or with a bigger group in a circle.

If there are just two players, dance around together for the first verse, let the child skip towards you for the second verse, suggest she does a little dance on the spot for the third verse, then dance around again together for the final verse.

If there is a group of children, choose a dancer to start in the centre and then get her to follow the actions suggested here.

(child stands in the middle while the others dance round her)

There's a brown girl in the ring,
Tra la la la la,
There's a brown girl in the ring,
Tra la la la la,
There's brown girl in the ring,
Tra la la la la,
For she like sugar and I like plum.

Then you skip across the ocean...
(child skips from one side of the circle to the other)

Then you show me your motion...
(child does a little dance move on the spot)

Then you show me your partner...
(everyone takes a partner and spins around)

Oranges and lemons

Age range 4+
Number of players Six or more
Energy level 2
What you will need No props

An update of the popular rhyme about the church bells of London, this version avoids the traditional 'chopping off' of the poor victim's head! The aim is to win the tug-of-war at the end.

How to play

Play this game on grass, so that no one hurts themselves in the final tug-of-war. Choose two tall children (or adults) to hold hands to make an arch. Privately, one of them chooses to be 'Oranges' and the other 'Lemons'.

All the other children line up in pairs in front of the arch, holding hands. As the song is sung they skip under the arch, then separate to go back down on either side of the arch-makers and skip back to the end of the line, where they join hands again to head towards the arch once more.

When the song gets to the final verse, 'Here comes a candle...', the two arch-makers draw their hands down between each pair until finally

one pair of children is caught on the last word 'OUT!'. The children then have to whisper either Oranges or Lemons to the arch-makers and go to stand behind the appropriate person.

At the very end of the game, when everyone is out and there are two long lines behind each arch-maker, there is a tug-of-war – which ends when one side falls over. The other side is then declared the winner.

Variation

If you want to avoid a boisterous tug-of-war, simply count how many children are behind each arch-maker at the end of the game. The one with the most children wins.

'Oranges and lemons,'
Say the bells of St Clement's.
'I owe you five farthings,'
Say the bells of St Martin's.
'When will you pay me?'
Say the bells of Old Bailey.
'When I grow rich,'
Say the bells of Shoreditch.
'When will that be?'
Say the bells of Stepney.

'I do not know,'
Says the great bell of Bow.
Here comes a candle to light you to
bed.
Here comes a giant with a
stomping tread.
Stomp, stomp, stomp, stomp
– you're OUT!

Tip for beginners

If it's hard to get a pair squeezing under the
arch, arrange the children in single file
instead.

Coming round the mountain

Age range 4+
Number of players Two or more
Energy level 3
What you will need No props

'She'll be coming round the mountain' is a well-known American folk song (reportedly either about a train or an early union organizer called 'Mother Jones'). It's become a campfire classic, so this action game is perfect for playing outside at any time.

How to play
Stand in a line or a circle and skip, while singing the song. When you get to 'Toot, toot!', mimic blowing a horn. Then stand with your hands on your hips and, moving from side to side, sing the chorus. Continue with different actions for each verse. All the players can break the circle and gallop around during the 'six white horses' verse, coming back together for the next chorus.

Variations
You can extend the song by inviting players to think of other ideas for what she'll be doing – such as 'wearing high-heeled boots' (all walk on tiptoe) or 'playing her fiddle' (mime playing a violin), and so on.

She'll be coming round the mountain
  when she comes!
She'll be coming round the mountain
  when she comes!
She'll be coming round the mountain
Coming round the mountain
Coming round the mountain
When she comes!
Toot, toot!

Chorus:
Singing ai-ai-yippee-yippee-ai
Singing ai-ai-yippee-yippee-ai
Singing ai-ai-yippee
Ai-ai-yippee
Ai-ai-yippee-yippee-ai.

Continue with the following verses:

She'll be riding six white horses
  when she comes... 'Whoa back!'
(pull on reins)

We'll all go out to meet her
  when she comes... 'Hiya Babe!'
(wave)

We'll all have chicken and dumplings
  when she comes... 'Yum, yum!'
(rub your tummy)

She'll be wearing pink pyjamas
  when she comes... 'Night night!'
(pretend to sleep)

The grand old Duke of York

Age range 3+
Number of players One or more
Energy level 2
What you will need No props

Even the youngest child will love this first marching game, which has lots of energetic variations to try. If several children are playing, they can all march in a line.

How to play
Sing the song and do the actions suggested.

The grand old Duke of York
(march on the spot)
He had ten thousand men,
(continue marching on the spot)
He marched them up to the top of the hill,
(march one way)
And then he marched them down again.
(turn round and march the other way)

And when they were up, they were up.
(march the original way)
And when they were down, they were down.
(march the other way again)
And when they were only halfway up,
(march on the spot)
They were neither up nor down!
(continue marching on the spot)

Variations
If you want to add more verses, change the third line with these suggestions:
* He skipped them up to the top of the hill
* He hopped them up to...
* He walked them up to...
* He danced them up to...
* They beat their drums to...
* They tooted their trumpets to...
* They blew their trombones to...

Tip for beginners
Have an adult leading the line, to make it easier for little ones to follow.

Mission impossible

Age range 5+
Number of players One or more
Energy level 3
What you will need A selection of sturdy, everyday household items, such as cardboard boxes, empty plastic bottles, an old sheet or groundsheet, upturned flowerpots; newspaper

This game uses lots of physical skills as children wriggle, jump, balance and run. It's designed to enable them to create and enjoy a mini-obstacle course, of which they can do one circuit or several. Before starting the game, make sure any items the players will stand on are sturdy and can take the child's weight. Check also for any sharp edges on boxes or flowerpots and clear the ground of twigs or stones that may cause scrapes.

Preparation

Arrange your equipment around the garden to create a circuit. For example, two open cardboard boxes that a child has to wriggle through like a tunnel, then a row of upright plastic bottles she must jump over without knocking them down, a sheet to crawl under, flowerpots to step across carefully, and a long,

thin strip of newspaper to walk along, balancing so that she doesn't touch the ground on either side. Mark the start and finish lines clearly with a strip of newspaper or a flag.

How to play

Make sure the children are wearing loose, comfortable clothing that's suitable for wriggling along the ground! Then line the first one up at the starting post. When you say 'Go!' she has to set off and complete the circuit as quickly as possible. Use a stopwatch if she enjoys the challenge of improving her time on subsequent circuits.

Variations
* If you've made a complicated course, mark each stage with a number, written clearly on a piece of paper.
* To extend the game, include some running within the course – for example, complete the circuit once, then run twice round the outside, then do another circuit.

Tips for beginners
• Arrange the obstacles in an obvious order – a circle or straight line – so that there's no confusion about which part of the course to tackle next.
• 'Walk' the course together, so that the child knows exactly where to go.

Snake race

Age range 3+
Number of players One or more
Energy level 2
What you will need A ball of string or wool; a child's bike, tricycle or toy car

This simple game can be adapted to any outdoor space where there's room to manoeuvre wheels, adding spice to a child's favourite ride-on toy – whether that's a bicycle, tricycle or toy car.

Preparation
Unravel the ball of string or wool and lay it down in a random pattern around the garden, ending back where you began. Cut the wool, then repeat the pattern with a parallel line, so that you've created a race track.

How to play
Get the child onto his bike or car and set him off along the race track, making sure that he stays on the 'road'.

Variations
* Start the ride with ten points. The child can gain extra points for completing the track without riding outside the marked area, or can lose them for straying off the road.
* Make the track more twisty and complicated for a more advanced rider.

Tip for beginners
To build confidence in a very young rider, set the track down where the child usually rides around, so that it's already familiar.

Age range 4+
Number of players One or more
Energy level 2
What you will need No props

Count me in

Adults can help with this game by counting along with the child and practising the steps together, before she goes it alone. It encourages counting skills as well as getting children moving.

Preparation
Go over the steps you'll be using in the game. These could include:

• Jumps
• Skips
• Hops
• Big steps
• Little steps
• Ballet leaps
• Sliding steps
• Star jumps

Tips for beginners
• Keep the number of instructions to a maximum of three, so that the child doesn't get confused.
• Help by counting along with her as she does each of the steps.

How to play
Start by asking the child to do one, two or more of any of the steps. Gradually build up the number and variety. There are three things for her to remember: *which* step, *how many* to do and *which order* they go in.

For example, you could start by saying:
'Do two big steps.'
Then move on to:
'Do two little steps and one jump.'
Then:
'Do one hop, three skips and one big step.'
Then:
'Do six jumps, two star jumps and one little step.'
And so on.

If she makes a mistake, she loses a point. If she gets them all right, she gains a point. If she's really good at this game, you might need to write down the instructions to remember the order in which you've asked them.

Then it's her turn to ask *you* to have a go!

Variations
* Ask the child to count aloud as she does each of the actions.
* Extend the game by including other instructions, such as: run to the fence and back; turn around; touch your toes. Older children might manage sit-ups or even press-ups as part of the routine.

Yo, heave-ho

Age range 5+
Number of players Possible with one, but best with two or more
Energy level 2
What you will need No props

'Yo, heave-ho' is suitable for any weather, although a blustery day is best, as the wind will give realistic on-board effects. And, even if your outdoor space is small, children's imagination can furnish lots of action in this adventure game.

Preparation

Get everyone to imagine they're about to set sail on a magnificent ship, with white sails billowing and the open seas ahead. Encourage children to talk about what the ship looks like: how the cabins might be furnished; the colour of the wood; how many ladders and masts there are on board; the oarsmen beneath the deck; and how the captain stands in command, turning the big wheel to steer his vessel.

Once everyone has a clear picture of the ship, you can start the game.

How to play

Tell the children they're hard-working sailors on board the ship. They have to do the actions for all the events that happen on board. For example, they must:

• *Swab the deck*
  (pretend cleaning with buckets and mops from side to side all over the garden)

• *Climb the rigging*
  (hand-over-hand actions, as if climbing a rope)

• *Bail out the boat, which has taken in water and is sinking*
  (pretend to empty lots of buckets overboard)

• *Help with the rowing*
  (sit down in a line and row in unison, counting each stroke)

• *Assist the captain in steering*
  (haul the wheel round in one direction, then the other)

You could also send them running up and down the deck to fetch ropes, jumping into the sea to rescue a man overboard, and so on.

Finally, night falls and the sailors can lie in their bunks for a rest!

Bowled over

Age range 5+
Number of players One or more
Energy level 1
What you will need A washing line, or similar; a selection of hoops; string; a beanbag

The aim of this game is to get a beanbag through a variety of different-sized hoops, which challenges children's accuracy and throwing skills. There are some variations that can make the game more difficult for accurate throwers.

Preparation

Put up a line at roughly eye level. It could be a washing line; or hang a skipping rope or some strong string between two supports.

Collect a selection of hoops: spinning rings, hoops from a stacking game or hula hoops; or cut out shapes from cardboard packets or boxes. You could even bend a wire coat hanger into a circular shape (don't let a child attempt this). Tie a string to each of the hoops and suspend them in a row along the line.

Mark a line at a reasonable distance from the row of hoops, behind which the child has to stand.

How to play

Ask the child to throw the beanbag, aiming to get it through the largest of the hoops. Count how many goes it takes before she's successful. Next, ask her to get the beanbag through each of the smaller hoops in succession. Keep a tally of the total number of goes it takes before all the hoops have been completed.

For the next round, see if the child can beat her last record.

Tip for beginners

Let the child stand right in front of the biggest hoop to begin with, gradually moving a step further back to make it a little harder after each successful throw.

Variations

* If a child's throws are very accurate, give her a handicap, such as throwing with her left hand if she's right-handed.
* Adjust the height of each hoop so that they aren't all at the same level.
* Tie other smaller targets to the line, such as a small toy or tightly screwed-up ball of newspaper, for precision practice.

Animal Olympics

Age range 3+
Number of players One or more
Energy level 3
What you will need Animal picture cards, or name cards; a few props, such as short bamboo canes, beanbags or other items that are to hand; a stopwatch may be useful

In this game children pretend to be a variety of strong, flexible or bouncy animals that are undoubted masters of their sporting abilities! It's a great opportunity for children to practise all sorts of physical skills.

Preparation

Cut out six pieces of paper or card and write an animal's name on each one. The child could do a picture on each card too, if he enjoys drawing. Decide on an event that would be suitable for each animal, such as:

- *Bunny*
  Hops over hurdles with ease

- *Monkey*
  Does astonishing gymnastics displays

- *Cheetah*
  Sprints into the lead in a short-distance race

- *Cat*
  Amazing balancing on the beam

- *Gorilla*
  The strongest weight-lifter

- *Horse*
  The best long-distance runner.

Variations

* Make more animal cards and ask the child to act out each one. See if you can guess which it is without being told. Then pick a picture yourself and do the same.
* Use a stopwatch and time some of the events, such as the sprint or long-distance race, to see if a child can improve his time.

Put all the name cards into a bag. Have some simple props to hand so that you can set up the appropriate items for whichever activity is picked.

How to play

The child chooses one of the cards from the bag (without peeking). If he chooses the powerful gorilla, you could put down a bamboo cane with a beanbag tied to each end to act as his weight-lifting challenge. He then has to raise it above his head to be declared the winner.

For the cheetah, mark a start and finish line. The bunny can hop over bamboo canes (raise them on flowerpots for more of a challenge) or pieces of string on the ground. Mark the four corners of the monkey's performing space – this is the child's chance to show off leaps, roly-polys, jumps and any other gymnastic skills. For the cat, set down two parallel lines of bamboo canes (or string), which the cat must stay inside while on the beam. Set the horse off on a steady trot, two, three, four or more times round the garden.

Once the child has completed one animal challenge, he chooses another from the bag until all six events are done.

> ### Tip for beginners
> Keep the activities very simple; for example, the bunny could simply hop ten times.

Dizzy snail trail

Age range 5+
Number of players One or more
Energy level 1
What you will need A ball of wool or string; a pebble or other weight

Challenge children's coordination skills and concentration with this game. It's lots of fun, and very easy to set up and put away too, which makes it useful when you need a diversion in a hurry.

Preparation

Secure the end of the ball of wool or string by putting a pebble (or similar) on it to make sure it doesn't move. Then gradually feed out the string in a large spiral shape, like a snail shell. Keep going round and round, making the spiral bigger, until you've made at least five or more rotations. Either cut off the string or put the ball down on the ground to mark the end of the course.

How to play

Get the child to start in the centre of the 'shell' and walk along the length of the string, without allowing his feet to step off on either side. He must follow the spiral round steadily until he reaches the end.

Tips for beginners

• Younger children can walk along the spiral pathway *between* the lines of string, rather than having to walk *on* it.
• If a child doesn't like feeling dizzy, make the string into a random wiggly pattern instead of a spiral. This way he can still enjoy following the line and challenging his balancing skills.

Variations

* Once he's reached the outside of the snail shell, the child has to turn round and carefully come back again, finishing the game at the centre.
* Try this as a speed race for an older child – how fast can he get along the spiral string without losing his balance and stepping off?
* Make the gaps between each spiral narrower, so that there are more of them – and a greater risk of getting dizzy and falling off!

Age range 5+
Number of players One or more
Energy level I
What you will need .Plastic cups; two plastic jugs

Fetch the water

Skill and a steady hand will prove essential in this game, the aim being to transport a jug full of water from one end of the garden to the other using a beaker – and spilling as little as possible.

Preparation
Mark a start and finish line, placing a jug full of water at the beginning and an empty jug at the end.

How to play
Fill a plastic cup or beaker with water and give it to the child. She has to walk or run to the finish line holding her cup of water, attempting to spill as little as possible. She pours it into the plastic jug, then runs back to you for a top-up. When she's emptied the full water jug, measure how much she's managed to pour into the jug at the finish line.

Variations
* The child can walk or run in zigzag lines.
* Make the course more complicated by setting out a longer circuit that goes all round the various parts of the garden. Mark the route with twig arrows or numbers written on pieces of paper.
* Time how long it takes her to transfer all the water from one jug to the next.

Tips for beginners
• Use a couple of drops of food colouring in the water so that it's easy for the child to see how much she's collected.
• Only fill the plastic cup half or three-quarters full, so that she's less likely to spill it en route.

Trail blazer

Age range 5+
Number of players One or more
Energy level 2
What you will need Pen and paper; an envelope; a small prize

This is a great problem-solving game and gives children a good run around, too! They have to solve an intriguing treasure hunt, which can be made harder or easier, depending on their ages.

Preparation

Cut out five or six pieces of paper and write a clue on each one. You may want to number them, as you need to make sure that each clue leads directly to the next one. For example, your first clue might read:

Down the path, behind the tree,
That's where your next clue will be!

Then hide clue two behind the tree, ready for him to find. Continue laying down clues all over the garden, until the final clue leads to the hiding place of the prize – perhaps a small toy or some wrapped sweets.

How to play

Put the first clue into the envelope, which you can deliver to the child; or write his name on the front and pretend it's just been delivered through the letterbox. When he opens it, help him decipher the clues and get going on the treasure trail. If outdoor space is limited, spread the clues through both house and garden, so that he gets a good run around as he chases after the trail.

Variations

* An older child may enjoy decoding more complicated clues, such as codes, anagrams or riddles. For example, 'Roll up to the top, then roll me back down' could be a clue hidden in a rolled-up curtain or blind at the top of the house.
* This game can encourage a very young child to read the clues himself, so keep them simple, such as, 'On top of the table' or 'Next to the bench'.

Tip for beginners

Draw a picture clue as well as the written one on each slip of paper, so that the child knows he's looking for a tree, bench, flowerbed, and so on.

1. Look behind the big tree!

Age range 4+
Number of players One or more
Energy level 2
What you will need Sheets of old
newspaper

Crocodile hop

An imaginative game that is easy to set up and bursting with energy. Children have to escape safely from the snapping crocs in a river by hopping over stepping stones to the security of an island.

Preparation

Tear the newspaper into sheets and arrange them at random around the garden. They represent the stepping stones in the river. In the centre, make a small 'island' with several sheets of newspaper. This will be 'home'.

How to play

The child is an intrepid explorer, investigating the river. Any area around the newspaper sheets is crocodile-infested water. The child starts off on the island, but then has to hop all over the stepping stones without falling into the 'water'. When you call out 'Crocodile!' she must jump back over the stones to the island as quickly as possible, to take refuge until you call out 'Crocodile clear!', when she can set off again.

Tip for beginners

Keep the newspaper stepping stones close to each other, so that it's easy for the child to move from one to the next.

Variation

Write big black numbers on each stepping stone, then call out numbers for the child to jump to.

Feeling hot, hot, hot

Age range 3+
Number of players One or more
Energy level 2
What you will need A small toy (perhaps a dog or a teddy) or a coin to hide

This very simple hide-and-seek game is especially popular with younger children, who can be encouraged with tips on how close they are to the prize and then rewarded with it, once they find it.

Preparation
While the child is not looking, hide a little toy or a coin in the garden.

How to play
Ask the child to look for the prize. If he finds it quickly, hide it again in a less obvious place. Once he starts having difficulty locating it, give clues such as *'You're getting hotter'* as he gets nearer; or *'You're getting colder'* as he moves further away.

If he's very close, say, *'You're boiling hot!'*

Tip for beginners
Before the game, make the toy have a little 'conversation' with the child, explaining that he's off to hide outside and hopes the child will find him soon.

Variation
For older children, explain that you're going to give 'opposite' clues. So if you say he's getting *hotter*, it actually means *colder*.

Age range 4+
Number of players Two or more
Energy level 2
What you will need Sticks, chalks or flowerpots; a small ball (the 'jack'); a beanbag for each person playing

Beanbag bowls

To play this game successfully requires an accurate aim, though younger children will simply enjoy the fun of learning to throw underarm and trying to hit the jack. The aim is to score the most points at the end of an agreed number of rounds by getting the beanbag as close as possible to the jack.

Preparation

Mark out a rough rectangle with sticks, chalks or corner markers, such as upturned flowerpots. Standing at one end, throw the small ball so that it lands within the rectangle.

How to play

Each person takes a turn to throw their beanbag at the jack, to try to get as close to it as they can. If the small ball is hit or moved, it is its final position at the end of the round that counts.

After the round is finished (when all the players have thrown their beanbags), the person with the beanbag closest to the jack scores one point and throws the ball for the next round, which is then played from the opposite end of the rectangle. The overall winner is the person with the most points at the end of an agreed number of rounds.

Variations
* Give each child more than one beanbag, so that they can throw two or more when it is their turn. But make sure you know which beanbags belong to which child!
* Instead of beanbags, try rolling soft balls towards the jack.

Tip for beginners
Rather than throwing the jack, place it down on the ground not too far away from the throwers, to make it an easier target.

First hopping fun

Age range 4+
Number of players One or more
Energy level 2
What you will need String; a small object such as a ring, ball or small toy; some plastic stacking beakers

Hopping isn't quite as easy as it looks – but young children will love the challenge once they have mastered the basic technique. This game teaches them how to hop with precision and control.

How to play

Explain that to hop, the child needs to take a little step, with one foot on the ground and the other foot in the air; then build up a series of steps on one foot. Once a child has got the knack of this, these easy games will help her gain confidence:

• Measure the child's height, then cut a piece of string to that length and lay it flat along the ground. Then ask her if she can 'hop her height' by hopping from one end of the string to the other. Then ask if she can hop twice her height/your height/the length of the garden fence.
• Mark a starting line with a horizontal stick and place your chosen object a few feet away (not too far or the challenge will be exhausting). From the starting line, ask the child to hop on one foot to the object, pick it up and then hop back on the other foot. If she puts her foot down on the ground, she has to go back to the starting line and begin again.
• Lay out a few upturned stacking beakers in a zigzag line and see if the child can weave her way around them while hopping.

Tip for beginners

If a child has never hopped before, begin by holding her hand gently to steady her. Then show her how to use her arms to help her balance herself.

Skipping without a rope

Age range 4+
Number of players One or more
Energy level 3
What you will need No props

Skipping is a great form of exercise for children and has a definite 'feel-good' factor. The aim of skipping without a rope is to practise the basic skill so that children can go on to skipping with a rope (see page 42) and other more advanced versions.

How to play

Explain that to skip, the child needs to take a little step and bounce on the foot she has down on the ground, then repeat this on the other foot until she builds up a rhythm. Practise maintaining a rhythm with her by chanting a rhyme while she skips, such as 'Lou, Lou, skip to my Lou' (see page 8). As with hopping, once a child can skip a few steps, a series of small challenges like the ones below will improve her technique:

• Develop control by playing 'Red, Amber, Green'. When you shout 'Red', the child must stop; when you shout 'Amber', she must walk; and when you shout 'Green', she must skip.
• Improve her concentration by mixing skipping with other physical skills, such as hopping, running, walking and jumping. In the park, get her to play some simple races, either with you or with another child, such as skipping to the tree and running back; hopping to a bench, skipping round it and jumping back; walking with giant steps to the end of the path, then skipping on the spot until you catch up.

Tip for beginners
Help new skippers to find their feet by skipping slowly alongside them.

Variation
Combine skipping with an imaginative game, such as pretending she is a bee fluttering from flower to flower, or a fairy escaping from a fearsome giant.

Hopscotch

Age range 7+
Number of players One or more
Energy level 2
What you will need A marker (such as a flat stone); some chalk; an even surface that you are allowed to mark with the chalk

This traditional and well-loved game is played in many different ways across the world. The aim is to complete the course (following the squares' numerical order) without stepping on the lines, falling over or putting your non-hopping foot down. If the marker is not thrown into the correct square, it must be thrown again.

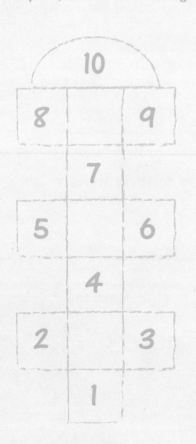

Preparation

Mark out the pavement (or other flat surface) in a rectangular grid in this way: one square, followed by two (or three) squares side by side, then one square, followed by two side by side, then one square, followed by two side by side, with a semicircle or square at the far end (see the diagram). Number the segments 1–10, with 1 being the nearest and 10 the semicircle.

How to play

Standing outside the square numbered 1, the player throws the marker into the first square and hops to 10 and back like this:

- Avoiding square 1 (where the marker is), she jumps over it and lands with one foot in square 2 and the other foot in square 3
- Then she hops onto square 4
- And jumps with both feet onto squares 5 and 6
- Now she hops onto square 7
- Then jumps with both feet onto squares 8 and 9
- And hops onto semicircle 10, where she turns around without putting her foot down
- Then she hops and jumps her way back to squares 2 and 3 – where she can bend down to pick up her marker from square 1
- And finally she hops into the now-empty square 1 and out of the grid entirely.

The next time round she throws her marker into square 2, and does the same moves, but this time avoids stepping on square 2 until she has picked her marker up on the way back down. She continues playing like this until she has thrown her marker into every square up to 10 and has hopscotched her way up and down the grid each time.

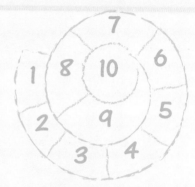

Variations

* Another way to play the game is to hop up – and into – the squares in turn, starting at 1, then pick up the marker, turn round and hopscotch back to the beginning from that square. For instance, if the marker has landed in square 5, the child will hop up and into square 5, stoop and pick up the marker, turn round, then hopscotch back to square 1 and out. In this version she only reaches square 10 on the very last go.
* Grids can be laid out in many different ways. Some may have squares 3 and 6 as singles, with 1/2, 4/5 and 7/8 side by side. Others may have diagonals dividing one large square into four triangles for the numbers 4, 5, 6 and 7 (see diagram). Or they might run in a spiral rather than a straight line (see diagram). Experiment with devising your own layout.
* Play the game with two or more children by taking turns after each throw. If the marker is not thrown into the correct square, that player misses her go.

Tips for beginners

* Instead of hopping, get children to jump into each square using both feet.
* Tell them to put both feet down in square 10 to make turning round easier.

Skipping with a rope

Age range 6+
Number of players One
Energy level 2
What you will need A skipping rope

Here's how to teach a child to skip with a rope, so that she can then go on to skip on her own or play some of the skipping rhyme games that children often play together in the school playground (see the ideas on pages 44–51).

How to play

Get the child to hold the rope in a loop behind her, standing straight and with her arms outstretched. The rope should just skim the ground behind her – if it's too long, wind the rope round her hands until it's the right length.

Then explain that to begin skipping, she needs to swing the rope over her head and jump over it in a small jump, with both feet off the ground. Get her to keep practising this until she has developed a steady rhythm.

Then try these ideas:

• Add a little hopping jump when the rope is overhead (double bounce)
• Jump on one foot
• Jump on alternate feet
• Skip forwards by taking steps on alternate feet
• Jump with the rope turning from front to back
• Go slower when you call 'Salt!' and faster when you call 'Pepper!'

Variations
* Try tapping first one foot, then the other one behind the opposite leg when the rope is overhead.
* Tap alternate heels in front instead.
* Jump the feet apart a little when the rope is overhead.
* Try crossing the arms in front as the rope comes down.

Tips for beginners
• Skip on a clear, flat surface.
• Make sure there is plenty of room.
• Perfect one skill before introducing a new one.

Skipping with friends

Age range 8+
Number of players Three or more
Energy level 3
What you will need A skipping rope long
enough to share

If skipping alone is fun, skipping in a
group is even more so... And there are
endless variations on the theme, using
different rhymes, varied formations and
different numbers of children.

How to play

Two people stand opposite each other and turn
the rope. The third person skips in the middle. He
may do this in two ways: either by skipping facing
the rope (as he would if he were skipping alone)
or by skipping parallel to it (that is, facing one of
the rope-turners).

When skipping parallel to the rope, it's best to
start with one child standing beside the rope
before it starts to turn. As the skipper becomes
more proficient, he will soon learn how to run
into the rope while it is turning (best done when
the rope touches the ground). Both running in
and running out take some practice, but when it's
mastered a whole line of children can run in and
out without the rope stopping turning at all.
Here's a rhyme to practise this:

Variation

If, rather than replacing each other at the
rope, several children want to skip together
in a long line, get them reciting a rhyme that
gradually introduces a new child with each
verse, such as this one:

I love the river, I love the sea,
(first child sings and skips)

I love Naomi skipping with me.
(second child comes in)

I love the river, I love the sea,
(Naomi now sings and skips)

I love Barney skipping with me
(third child comes in)

And so on.

Mother's in the kitchen
(child skips)

Doing all the stitching
(child skips)

In comes the pussycat
(child points to or names the next person)

And shoos her OUT
(new person comes in and original child goes out)

Age range 7+
Number of players Three
Energy level 3
What you will need A long skipping rope

Bubble car

Children can practise stopping the rope with this 'round the corner' game, in which the aim is to skip out and then back in again – and bring the rope to a standstill.

How to play
Two people turn the rope for the skipper, who sings the rhyme below and follows the actions.

I'm a little bubble car, Number 48
(child skips over the rope)

I whizz round the coooooorner
(child runs out of the rope, around one of the rope-turners and back in on the other side)

And slam on the brakes!
(child raises only one foot as the rope comes round, then stamps that foot down so the rope is trapped between his feet)

Variation
Rather than the skipper being a car, get him to try being an aeroplane (with his arms held out as 'wings') or a bicycle (make cycling movements with his arms).

Tips for beginners
• Get children to practise stopping the rope a couple of times before chanting the whole rhyme.
• Remind them not to run too fast when they are 'whizzing round the corner' in case they fall over.

Teddy bear, teddy bear

Age range 6+
Number of players Three or more
Energy level 3
What you will need A long skipping rope

This nursery rhyme is better known as a skipping game in which the players do all the actions and then complete as many continuous skips as possible.

How to play

Two people turn the rope, while the third skips in the middle. The two rope-turners chant the rhyme while the skipper follows the suggested actions. If she successfully completes the whole verse, the skipper does as many continuous skips as she can (without bouncing in between) while the rope-turners count them. As soon as there is a stumble, a new game begins and the rope-turners become skippers.

Tips for beginners
• Turn the rope slowly.
• Instead of turning around on the second line, mime tracing a circle.

Variations
If there are several children playing, start with a single child skipping, then begin the rhyme again with a second person running in to join her, then a third, and so on.

Teddy Bear, Teddy Bear
(skip with bounces in between)

Turn around,
(turn in a circle)

Teddy Bear, Teddy Bear
(skip with bounces in between)

Touch the ground,
(bend down to touch the ground)

Teddy Bear, Teddy Bear
(skip with bounces in between)

Climb the stairs,
(lift knees to mime climbing the stairs)

Teddy Bear, Teddy Bear
(skip with bounces in between)

Say your prayers,
(bend head and put hands together)

Teddy Bear, Teddy Bear
(skip with bounces in between)

Turn off the light,
(mime pulling a light cord)

Teddy Bear, Teddy Bear
(skip with bounces in between)

Say 'Goodnight!'
(children all shout GOODNIGHT)

Age range 8+
Number of players At least six
Energy level 2
What you will need A very long
skipping rope

All in together

This is a great game if a large number of children are playing together. They are trying to get to 'December' with everybody skipping in a line and without the rope ever having stopped turning.

How to play
Two people turn the rope. The others all stand in a line to one side, in the order of the month of their birth, with January at the head. As the rope-turners chant the rhyme below, the others gradually run in to skip, as the appropriate month of their birth is called out.

All in together, girls.
Never mind the weather, girls.
When I say your birthday, please run in.
January... February... March...
April... May... June... July... August...
September... October... November...
DECEMBER!

Variations
* If just boys are playing, replace 'girls' with 'boys'; if both boys and girls are playing, replace 'girls' with 'mates'.
* Play the game using children's names instead of birthdays – just swap 'birthday' with 'letter' and the months of the year with letters of the alphabet.

Tip for beginners
Let the children have a few practice tries at running into the rope before beginning the rhyme properly.

Who will I marry?

Age range 10+
Number of players Three
Energy level 3
What you will need A skipping rope

This game is intended to predict the name of the boy or girl whom the skipper will marry in the future. It's often a cause of great hilarity and speculation among the children playing it.

How to play
Two children turn the rope while the third skips. As the rope-turners turn, they chant the rhyme below. When the skipper eventually stumbles, the letter being chanted as she stops becomes the initial of her boyfriend's name, which is then chosen by the other two children – usually amid much giggling.

Variations
* If boys are playing, replace 'her boyfriend' with 'his girlfriend'.
* If you don't feel K-I-S-S-I-N-G is appropriate, change it to H-U-G-G-I-N-G or even T-A-L-K-I-N-G.

[child's name] is with her boyfriend
Sitting in a tree
K-I-S-S-I-N-G!
They're getting married,
Who could it be?
Their name begins with...
A, B, C, D, E, F, G, etc.

Age range 8+
Number of players Three or more
Energy level 3
What you will need A circular elastic rope (or similar, made by looping large elastic bands together and tying them in a knot at the end to create a circle of elastic)

French skipping

Rather than using an ordinary skipping rope, this game uses a stretchy 'rope', which is held in place around the rope-holders' ankles. The aim is for the skipper to do the moves and chant a rhyme, while the stretchy rope is held at a low level.

How to play
The two rope-holders stand inside the circular rope with their feet apart. Holding it behind their ankles, they pull the rope into a rectangular shape. The skipper starts with both feet on the outside of the rope and, chanting a rhyme of his choice, jumps in and out of the rectangle in time with the rhyme. The steps get more complex as the skipper gets better.

Variations
* The skipper begins with both feet inside the rectangle, then jumps over the outside of the rope with either one foot or both, and back in again.
* Standing with both feet outside, the skipper jumps and loops the near-side rope over the far-side rope, tapping his foot, then jumps back to the start.
* The rope-holders move the rope higher up their legs to make the game harder.

Tip for beginners
Get novices to jump behind someone who already knows the moves and copy them.

Double Dutch

Age range 10+
Number of players Three or more
Energy level 3
What you will need Two long skipping ropes of the same length

A highly skilled skipping game, this uses two ropes and requires precision timing – both from the skipper and from those turning the rope. It's likely to take a lot of practice, but the sense of achievement will be great.

Tip for beginners
Make sure that any child who tries this is totally confident skipping with a single rope.

How to play
The two rope-holders have a rope in each hand and turn one clockwise and the other anticlockwise, so that one rope is in the air while the other is on the ground. This isn't easy, and it will take considerable practice to establish a regular rhythm.

Once the ropes are turning evenly, the skipper runs in from one end and, hopping from one foot to another, quickly skips over one rope and then the other. To leave the ropes, she runs out past a rope-holder.

Variation
Experienced Double Dutch skippers can try adapting their favourite single rope moves to the double ropes.

Age range 7+
Number of players One or more
Energy level 3
What you will need A skipping rope

Cinderella

'Cinderella' is a very popular skipping game that is played in many school playgrounds. Players count the highest number of 'disgusted people' they can! There are many variations, with different numbers of players, actions and rhymes.

How to play

Skip to the rhyme below with double bounces. Then, when the number section is reached, change to single bounces and try to count as high as possible without stumbling.

Cinderella dressed in yella
Went to town to meet a fella.
On the way her girdle busted –
How many people were disgusted?
I, 2, 3, 4, 5, etc.

Variations

* Play this as a group skipping game by adding new people into the line when the counting section starts (stick to double bounces in this case).
* This game can also be played as a clapping game. Facing a partner, clap first with one hand, then with the other and then with both. Skilled clappers can add in their own moves, too.
* There are many alternative rhymes for this game. Here is one of them:

Cinderella dressed in yella
Went to town to meet a fella.
By mistake she kissed a snake,
How many doctors did it take?
I, 2, 3, 4, 5, etc.

Tip for beginners

Novice skippers will find it easier to stick to double bounces for the counting section, rather than attempting fast single bounces.

Hot potato

Age range 8+
Number of players Two or more
Energy level I
What you will need A tennis ball

Players need to be pretty confident about their catching skills for this game, as it involves throwing, catching and keeping in the air a 'hot potato' while on the run, without dropping it.

How to play

The first player picks up the ball – the 'hot potato' – and throws it up and down. He then throws it to another player, who must catch it, but isn't allowed to hold it for more than a second at a time. He then throws it to another player, and so on, until one player drops the hot potato or holds it for too long.

Tip for beginners

The player with the hot potato calls out the name of the player he's going to throw it to, to give them time to prepare for a catch.

Variations

* To make the game more challenging, the players all have to run around as they throw and catch the hot potato.
* Use a chestnut or a small bouncy ball instead of a tennis ball.

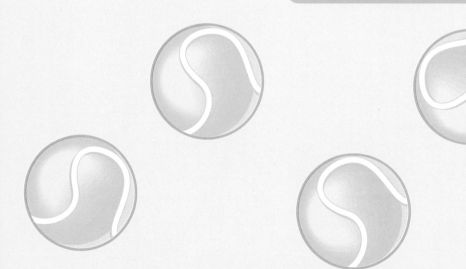

Age range 7+
Number of players One or more
Energy level 2
What you will need Football coaching markers, or a selection of twigs or stones to act as markers; a stopwatch or watch with a second hand

Weaving wonders

This game encourages physical coordination and speed – the aim being to weave in and out of a series of markers placed on the ground as accurately and speedily as possible, in the style of slalom skiing.

Preparation
Lay down the markers in a long row, allowing 1 m (3 ft) or so between each one.

How to play
Start the stopwatch and the first player sets off, weaving in and out of the markers, working from left to right. At the end of the row she turns around and runs back in a straight line alongside the markers to the finish.

Any remaining players take turns to do the course, and make a note of their times. When everyone has had a rest, they do the course again and see if any players have improved their times. If there is only one player, she will be competing against her own previous times.

Variations
* Devise a more complicated pattern for the players to follow – for example, weaving in and out of one marker, then leaving two, then one again, and so on.
* If players aren't too dizzy, they can weave in and out of the markers on the return journey as well.

Tips for beginners
• Leave a bigger space between the markers to make it easier for younger players.
• Use fewer markers.

Dodge that ball

Age range 8+
Number of players Six or more
Energy level 2
What you will need A soft ball

A favourite of school sports teachers, this game translates easily into the park – and is great for larger groups. Players try to hit the other team's members with the ball and get them out.

Preparation
Divide the players into teams. Each team lines up in a row, and the teams then face each other. There should be a space of at least 2–3 m (7–10 ft) between teams, with a dividing line between them (this can be imaginary, or can be marked out with leaves or twigs if necessary).

How to play
One person on the first team throws the ball underarm towards the opposing team, trying to hit a member of that team below the knees.

If they score a valid hit below the knee, that player is captured and has to cross the line and stand behind the first team.

Then the second team has a turn at throwing the ball. They can try to hit it over the team, so that their captured player catches it and is allowed to escape, or they can try to hit members of the opposing team and take their own prisoners.

The winning team is the first to capture all the other team members, or the team with the most prisoners after a time limit.

Tip for beginners
Use a larger – but still soft – ball to make the game easier.

Stuck in the mud

Age range 4+
Number of players Four or more
Energy level 3
What you will need No props

This energetic chasing and catching game requires lots of cooperation for it to continue! Players try to keep moving themselves and at the same time help their team-mates escape from being stuck fast in the mud.

How to play
You (or a nominated player) are the 'baddie' while all the others are on the same team.

The players all run away from the baddie, who has to try to touch as many of them as possible. If the baddie succeeds in touching a player, that player has to stand still with his legs wide apart – stuck in the mud.

He is not allowed to move again until one of his team-mates crawls through his legs to free him. If someone is caught trying to rescue a team-mate, then that player must also stand stuck in the mud.

The game continues until all the players are stuck in the mud – or until the baddie can no longer catch any of them!

Tip for beginners
The baddie can allow stuck players to escape after being in the mud for 30 seconds, if no one is able to rescue them.

Variations
* To make it harder, the rescuer has to crawl in a figure of eight around the stuck player's legs before that player is rescued from the mud.
* If the ground you're playing on is too hard or wet for crawling, devise another method for releasing stuck players, such as the rescuer holding their hands and the pair swinging round in a full circle together, or jumping up and down together holding hands three times.

Colourful croc

Age range 3+
Number of players Two or more
Energy level 1
What you will need No props

This is a simple game with an element of danger that the youngest players can enjoy. They are attempting to travel safely to the fairy's castle on the far side of the river, without Mr Croc getting his teeth into them.

Variation

For players who don't find fairies appealing, change the rhyme to:

*Swim across the water
A knight upon his charger.
What colour will he wear?*

How to play

One player, chosen as the crocodile, stands on one side of an imaginary line, guarding a fairy castle (a tree or bush), while the other players line up opposite.

The players who want to visit the fairy who lives on the other side of the river all chant together:

*Swim across the water
To see the fairy daughter.
Which colour will she wear?*

The crocodile then takes a good look at all the players and calls out a colour, such as 'Pink!'.

Any player who is wearing pink must then try to cross to the other side without being caught by the crocodile. Anyone who is caught becomes the next crocodile.

Tip for beginners

If all the players are wearing similar colours, the crocodile can pick out one particular player by saying, 'He'll wear the same blue shirt as... [name of player]!' Then that person has to try to cross the river.

Age range 7+
Number of players One or more
Energy level 2
What you will need A selection of football coaching markers or other items to act as markers and obstacles; a bike or skateboard

Rally cross

Setting up an obstacle course is easy in a wide open space, and can give even experienced riders or skaters a fresh challenge. The intention is to get round the course accurately – and without falling over!

Variation
If players are confident riders, set up your obstacle course on an area where there's a slight slope, to add extra interest.

Preparation
Set up an obstacle course using the markers, for the players to cycle or skate around.

How to play
Players have to complete the course successfully. Try these ideas:

• Weaving in and out of the markers
• Riding around a group of trees
• Riding along a straight line
• Riding to make 'shapes', such as a triangle, square or rectangle.

Follow my leader

Age range 3+
Number of players Two or more
Energy level 2
What you will need No props necessary, but you may like to include a few, such as a ball or ribbons

This copying game can be as energetic as you like. Players have to follow their leader's actions, and then think of their own when they get a turn as leader.

How to play

Players line up behind a leader. The leader then sets off at a jogging pace and the players follow in a line behind, singing this song:

We're following the leader
The leader, the leader,
We're following the leader
Wherever she may go.

Then the leader begins an action. For example, she might start to hop like a frog, or run madly in a zigzag line. The other players imitate the action, still following behind.

After a while the leader stops the action and goes back to an ordinary jog again. Then the followers begin the song again and wait for the next action. This might be something along the lines of:
• Flying like a plane, running along fast with arms outstretched
• Zooming along like a car, holding an imaginary steering wheel
• Chuffing along in a train, with arms making wheel movements.

Variation

After each action has finished, the leader goes to the back of the line, allowing the next in line to be leader.

Tips for beginners

• To make it easier, the leader can face the players to show them the action and make sure they understand how to do it, before turning round and leading them on.
• The leader can ask the players if they can guess what the action is meant to be, before they begin it themselves.

Please, Mr Policeman

Age range 4+
Number of players Three or more
Energy level 2
What you will need No props

Most children will love this game, where Mr Policeman gets to be the boss and makes all the decisions – but keep an eye out to make sure that no child is being unfairly penalized!

Tips for beginners
• Very young children will need an adult to be Mr Policeman.
• If they are finding it hard to think of different ways of moving, give the children some suggestions to pick from: hops, skips, jumps, fairy steps, sideways crab steps, leaps, giant strides or tippytoes steps.

Preparation
With a few twigs, mark out a starting line and a finishing line some way apart.

How to play
Players choose one person to be Mr Policeman, who then stands behind the finishing line. The others all stand in a row behind the starting line.

The first person – say, Fiona – starts the game by saying,
'Please, Mr Policeman, may I take two big hops?'
(or some other choice).

Mr Policeman then answers in one of the following ways:
• *'Yes, Fiona, you may take two big hops'*
• *'No, Fiona, you may not take two big hops'*
• *'No, Fiona, you may not take two big hops – but you may take one long stride'*
  (or some other choice).

Fiona then has to say, *'Thank you, Mr Policeman'*, and do whatever movement Mr Policeman has said she may do. If she forgets to say *'Thank you'*, or does the wrong movement, she has to go back behind the starting line.

The play moves on to the next person, who asks their request. The game continues in this way until one person eventually crosses the finishing line and becomes the new Mr Policeman.

Snake chase

Age range 6+
Number of players Five or more
Energy level 3
What you will need No props

In this game children switch from being free runners to being part of a long catching 'snake'. If several children are playing, the snake can get rather unwieldy, so for safety, play the game on soft grass. The aim is to be the last person to be caught.

Tip for beginners

Tell the children that the players at *both* ends of the snake can catch a new person, which makes it easier to tag them.

How to play

The children choose who will be It. He then covers his eyes and counts to 10, while all the other players run away. Once It has finished his countdown, he chases everyone else until he eventually catches someone.

This person now join hands with It and runs with him to catch a third person, who then joins the line. As more and more people are caught, the line becomes a long 'snake'. The last player left uncaught wins the game and becomes the new It.

Variation

Add another element to the game by allowing anyone who is touching wood, such as a tree, fence or bench, to be safe from being caught by the snake. They may only touch wood for a count of three, though, after which they must run around again.

Tree, bench, home

Age range 4+
Number of players Four or more
Energy level 3
What you will need A few trees and a park bench; something to mark 'home'

This game needs an adult to call out the instructions, as well as to judge who is in and who is out, as players try to stay in the game for as long as possible without being called 'out'.

Preparation

Choose a place in the park that has some trees and at least one bench. Then mark out a spot as 'home' – using a picnic rug, a log or a pile of sweaters – a little way from the trees or bench.

How to play

When you call out 'Run!' everyone runs around until you shout out another instruction: 'Tree!', 'Bench!' or 'Home!'.

• **Tree**
Everyone has to run and find a tree to touch (one person per tree). If someone fails to find a tree before you count to three, they are out.

• **Bench**
Everyone has to run to a bench and sit on it with their feet off the ground (sitting on laps is allowed). If they don't get to the bench before you count to three, or there is no room on it or their feet touch the ground, they are out.

• **Home**
Everyone has to run to home and touch it. If they cannot reach it before you count to three, they are out.

You then shout *'Run!'* once more and the game begins again. The last person in is the winner.

Tips for beginners

• Count up to three more slowly if you sense that a younger child is having difficulty getting to a target.
• Allow more than one person per tree.
• For safety, set a clear boundary, beyond which no one is allowed to run – such as 'up to the path, but no further'.

Variation

Adapt the instructions to suit the environment. For instance, if there isn't a bench, choose another landmark, such as a wall ('Wall!') or tennis-court net ('Net!').

Home corner

Age range 6+
Number of players Four or more
Energy level 3
What you will need Several trees, bushes or park benches that are well spaced apart – these are the 'home corners'

This game is an outdoor version of musical chairs – on a much bigger scale. Players try to get back to one of the home corners before the other players beat them to it.

Preparation

Decide which trees, bushes or benches are going to be your 'home corners'. If there are four players, there should be three home corners – that is, one fewer than the number of players. Make sure they are all at roughly the same distance from the players' starting area.

How to play

The players all gather and hold hands, dancing round in a circle together. Alternatively they can jump on the spot or jog round in a circle. As long as they are all together, no one player has an unfair advantage.

You should either sing or beat time with a stick on the ground, to act as the music. When you stop, the players all have to dash to reach the safety of a home corner. This means that one player will be left without a home and is called out. The other players come back to the centre and the game begins again, this time minus one home corner.

The last round will be between two players aiming for the final home corner – whoever gets there first wins!

Variations

* To be scrupulously fair about distances, you can position your own markers at, say, thirty paces from the centre.
* If two players reach a home corner simultaneously, they have to run back to the starting point – whoever gets back first is the winner of that home corner.

Tip for beginners

You can handicap older or faster players by making them stay in the centre of the playing area for a few seconds, while younger ones get a head-start once the music has stopped.

Age range 7+
Number of players Three or more
Energy level 2
What you will need A plastic bucket of
water; one or more cheap bath sponges

Splashing sponges

This is a very silly game that's strictly for
hot days only – when it has a refreshing,
cooling effect! The aim is to get your
opponent wet and to remain dry
yourself, though usually everyone gets
soaked by the end.

How to play
One player is the baddie, armed with a wet
sponge. She chases the other players and has to
hit one of them with the sponge. The wet player
then becomes the baddie and tries to hit another
player, topping up the sponge with cold water
from the bucket as necessary.

Variation
Older players may enjoy making this a
'paintball'-style game, with all players armed
with wet sponges and creeping up on each
other to strike from hidden positions.

Tips for beginners
• Use small sponges or small, soft sponge
  balls for younger players, so the 'impact'
  isn't as strong.
• Warm water makes it a gentler game, too.

Dog and bone

Age range 7+
Number of players Six or more
Energy level 2
What you will need An object such as a beanbag, sponge ball or soft toy to act as the bone

All children love 'tag' games, and this one can be played wherever there is some open space. The more participants, the merrier, although an even number of children is best.

Preparation
Pick the object to be the 'bone'. Divide the children into two teams, each of which allocates all its members a different number, starting with 1, 2, 3, etc. This must be done in secret so that the members of each team don't find out who on the opposite team has the same number as them.

How to play
The teams line up at opposite ends of the playing area. Place the bone equidistant between them and call out a number.

The child with that number from each team has to run out, grab the bone and return it to his side. The player who manages to do this first gains a point for his team. While the child is carrying the bone, his opponent is free to try and tag him; if he succeeds, his own team wins the point.

You then put the bone back into play and call the other numbers out until they have all been called, when the points are added up and the winning team is announced.

Tip for beginners
Another member of the team, whose number has *not* been called, might pretend to run forward, tricking the opposition and allowing their own player to perform a surprise tag.

Variations
* Players who are tagged have to drop the bone immediately. Neither player can tag the other until one of them has picked the bone up again, and the first player back to his team with the bone wins the point.
* After a few goes, the referee can call two or more numbers together, or call out some mental arithmetic, such as '6 minus 4, then add 1'.

Age range 3+
Number of players Three or more
Energy level 2
What you will need A basket or box;
different-coloured balls or other small objects

Hen and eggs

This game for younger children is guaranteed to produce lots of screams and excitement. It's a good way to teach them colours and will help to improve their coordination and throwing skills.

How to play

One player is the hen and covers her eyes some distance away from the other players, who each steal an 'egg' from the basket.

When everyone has chosen, the hen calls out a colour. All those holding eggs of that colour have to return them to the basket without being tagged by the hen.

Anyone who is tagged is out of the game. The last person to be caught is the winner.

Variation

Players can try throwing their eggs into the basket without being tagged by the hen.

Tip for beginners

Younger players will find it easier to start with just one egg. Once they have got the hang of the game, they can progress to picking several, which can be stuffed into pockets while they run.

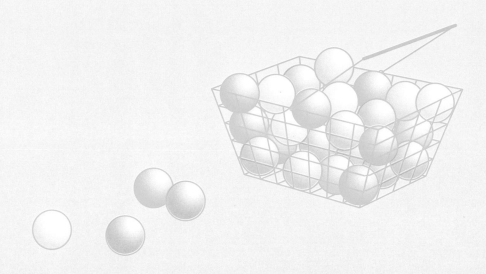

Pass it round

Age range 5+
Number of players Two or more
Energy level I
What you will need A cricket bat (a light plastic one is best for young players); a small soft ball

This simple version of a park favourite (also known as French cricket) can be played by a twosome, though it's more fun as a team game. The aim is to score runs and not get caught out.

Variations

* Decide on boundaries – if the batter hits the ball beyond the agreed boundary, he scores six runs.
* Allow the bowler to use false starts to try to trick the other player into lifting the bat and exposing their shins.

Tip for beginners

Novices can play the game simply as a 'hit your legs' challenge without runs, until they are really confident about batting and bowling the ball.

How to play

One player is chosen to be the batter, the other to be the bowler. If there are several players, they can be divided into two teams. The batter holds the cricket bat in front of his legs. The bowler then throws the soft ball underarm, trying to hit the batter's shins.

If the batter hits the ball, the bowler (or fielders, if there are other team members) runs to get it. Meanwhile, the batter passes the bat round his tummy, scoring a 'run' each time.

The batter is out if:

• The bowler catches the ball after the batter has hit it, without it bouncing
• The bowler manages to hit the batter's shins while bowling the ball.

Roll around

Age range 3+
Number of players Four or more
Energy level 1
What you will need A large soft ball

This is a very simple game that is ideal for pre-schoolers and their parents. Play should continue until everyone has had a turn at catching the ball and calling out the name of the next person to receive it.

How to play

Get everyone to sit in a circle and give the ball to one person (a grown-up may be best to begin with). She chooses someone else in the circle, calls out his name and then rolls the ball gently towards him. When the child whose name was called out has received the ball, he chooses a new child, calls out her name and rolls the ball towards her. The game continues like this until everyone has had at least one go of calling and rolling the ball.

Tip for beginners
Little ones are not always great at aiming the ball correctly, so get them to look directly at the child who is going to receive the ball before they actually begin rolling it.

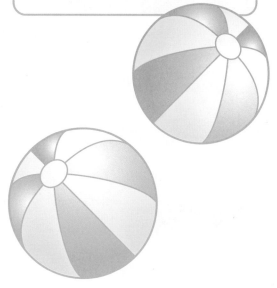

Variations
* Older children can stand in a ring and throw the ball to each other.
* Speed up the time between throws.
* To make the game harder, don't call out the names to give warning who you're throwing to next.

The aim game

Age range 3+
Number of players One or more
Energy level 1
What you will need A bucket and a collection of small balls, such as tennis balls, bouncy balls or table-tennis balls

Young children will love this simple target-practice game, while older children can enjoy a more demanding variation. Players are trying to get as many balls into the bucket as they can.

How to play

Place the bucket upright on the ground, then let the child stand by it and take five steps backwards. Give her as many small balls as you have, and ask her to try to throw them – one at a time – into the bucket. For each ball that she successfully gets in, she scores one point.

When all the balls have gone, it's your turn (or another child's turn). If anyone manages to get all the balls into the bucket in one go, she takes another step backwards for the next round of the game.

The player with the most points at the end wins. Try playing 'best of' three or five rounds.

Variations

* If you are playing with children of different ages, handicap the older ones by positioning them further away from the bucket, or by telling them to throw with one hand behind their back.
* For more competitive older children, mark out a line with set points along the way. Starting from the point nearest the bucket, each child takes turns to throw a ball into it. When they get one in, they move back down the line to the next point. The first person to get all the way to the end of the line is the winner.
* Turn the bucket on its side and roll the balls into it, rather than throwing them. Allow a point for every ball that goes in, even if it rolls out again.

Tips for beginners
• Stand younger children even closer to the bucket.
• Give little ones juggling balls or beanbags to throw with, because they are easier to aim accurately.

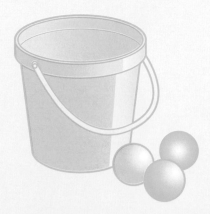

Age range 7+
Number of players Two or more
Energy level I
What you will need Cardboard boxes;
three soft small balls; a scorecard

Box drop

Although similar to 'The aim game' (see
opposite), this game is more demanding
because it requires accuracy and scoring
skills. Players have to try and throw their
balls into the highest-scoring boxes to
win the greatest number of points.

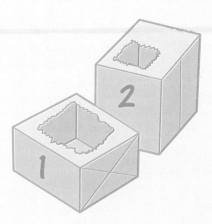

Preparation
Collect as many cardboard boxes as you can (at
least three) and seal them shut. Then cut out
different-sized holes in each one, going from large
to small. Now write the score points on the
boxes, with the largest hole having the lowest
score (I) and the smallest hole having the highest.

Line up the boxes with the higher-scoring ones
in the middle and the lower-scoring ones at the
edge. Mark out a line behind which the throwers
must stand.

How to play
Taking turns, each player throws three balls at the
boxes. Any ball that lands inside a box scores the
number of points written on that box. Scores are
recorded on the scorecard at the end of each go.

At the end of an agreed number of turns, the
total scores are added up and the winner is the
one with the most points.

Tips for beginners
• When there are children of different ages
  and abilities playing, have several lines
  behind which they must stand, to even up
  the competition.
• Make sure the ball can definitely fit
  through the smallest hole!

Variation
If you have several cardboard boxes, rather
than lining them up in a row, arrange them
in a cluster so that they are two (or even
three) layers deep.

Piggy in the middle

Age range 4+
Number of players Three
Energy level 2
What you will need A medium-sized ball

A favourite playground game – but watch to make sure that no one gets left in the middle for too long, or there'll be tears! Players need to be fair in giving the 'piggy' a chance to catch the ball, by not throwing it too high. This game is ideal for any outside play, including the beach, and can even be enjoyed in the shallows or at the swimming pool, under adult supervision.

Variations
* Try rolling the ball along the ground instead of throwing it.
* If there are several children, play the game standing in a circle with a couple of 'piggies' in the middle.

How to play
The three players line up in a row. The two outside players throw the ball to each other, while the middle one – the 'piggy' – tries to intercept it. If he does intercept it successfully, he then swaps places with the person who threw it, and that person then becomes the piggy in the middle.

The game is open-ended and finishes when everyone has had a turn at being the piggy.

Tip for beginners
Throw the ball quite low down, so that it's easier for shorter children to intercept it.

Age range 5+
Number of players Three or more
Energy level 2
What you will need A plastic bat (any kind will do); a foam ball

Bat that!

This first bat-and-ball game has easy-to-learn rules, making it a good starter ball game for young children. The aim is for players to win the right to be the batter as often as possible.

Tip for beginners
Use big bats and balls for young children.

How to play

Choose one player to be the batter – all the others are fielders. The batter hits the ball towards the fielders, then places the bat on the ground and stands still. Meanwhile the fielders try to catch the ball.

If someone catches the ball without it dropping on the ground, she automatically swaps places with the batter. If someone catches the ball after it has bounced, or just picks it up from the ground, she has to roll it back towards the bat.

If the rolling ball hits the bat, the person who rolled it swaps places with the batter. If it doesn't hit the bat, the original batter has a second go.

Simon says

Age range 6+
Number of players Four or more
Energy level 2
What you will need A small ball for every child playing

You can adapt this well-known action game to focus on improving ball skills. As in the traditional version, players have to do what Simon says – and *not* do anything he doesn't say!

How to play

Give each child a ball and choose one to be 'Simon'. Simon then tells the children an action that they should do with their balls and demonstrates it himself. Usually he prefaces his commands with 'Simon says...' – but sometimes

'Simon says throw the ball up in
the air and catch it with one hand'

he doesn't. The children must listen carefully and only do the actions that begin with 'Simon says...'

Any command that isn't prefaced with 'Simon says...' should be ignored and the children should just stand still. Those who forget to do so are out. The last one left in is the winner.

Actions to try

Not sure what actions to suggest? Try these:
* Throw the ball from one hand to the other
* Throw the ball up in the air and catch it with both hands
* Throw the ball up in the air and catch it with one hand
* Throw the ball up in the air and catch it with the other hand
* Throw the ball up in the air and clap before catching it
* Throw the ball up in the air and clap twice before catching it
* Throw the ball under one leg and catch it
* Bounce the ball on the ground while standing still
* Bounce the ball on the ground while moving along
* Pass the ball around your body
* Roll the ball along the ground
* Dribble the ball along the ground with your foot.

Tips for beginners

• If there are children who haven't played 'Simon says' before, have a warm-up game of the traditional version first. (This is where Simon just gives simple actions to do, such as jumping, hopping, turning around, touching their nose or waving their hands in the air.)
• If you haven't enough balls, team the children into pairs, with one ball between two, and let them throw to each other.

Queen-i-o

Age range 7+
Number of players Four or more
Energy level 2
What you will need A small ball

This game of bluff works best with several children, but smaller groups will still enjoy it. The aim is to guess who is hiding the ball, so as to enjoy more time as 'Queen-i-o'.

Variations
* When it's a boy's turn to be the thrower, change the name to 'King-i-o'.
* Instead of players hiding the ball in their hands behind their back, they can hide it elsewhere – up a jumper, tucked into the back of a sock or squeezed between the knees – and do the following actions while chanting the rhyme:

Queen-i-o,
(point towards the thrower once)
Queen-i-o,
(point towards the thrower a second time)
Who's got the ball-i-o?
(make a ball-shaped circle with their hands)
I haven't got it,
(point to themselves)
It isn't in my pocket,
(mime emptying out pockets)
So Queen-i-o,
(point towards the thrower)
Queen-i-o,
(point towards the thrower again)
Who's got the ball-i-o?
(make a ball-shaped circle with their hands)

How to play
One person is given the ball and goes to stand a little way off from all the other players. Facing away from them and calling, 'Ready, Steady, *Throw!*', she throws the ball backwards over her shoulder for one of the children to catch.

The child who catches the ball must quickly hide it behind his back. Then all the other children put their hands behind their backs in a similar way, stand in a line and chant the rhyme, opposite.

When they have finished chanting, the thrower must turn round and select the person she thinks has the ball. If she's wrong, that person then becomes Queen-i-o, and the thrower goes back to join the other children. If she's right, she continues being Queen-i-o for the next round.

Queen-i-o, Queen-i-o,
Who's got the ball-i-o?
I haven't got it,
It isn't in my pocket.
So Queen-i-o, Queen-i-o,
Who's got the ball-i-o?

Tip for beginners
Young children may find it hard to throw the ball very far over their shoulder, so keep the others quite close behind.

Upsy-downsy

Age range 5+
Number of players Two or more
Energy level 1
What you will need A small ball

This throw-and-catch game of forfeits is best played on a grassy surface to protect the children's knees. They're trying to catch the ball without dropping it and, in doing so, avoid the forfeits.

How to play

Position the children so that there is a reasonable space between them. Give the ball to one child and ask him to throw it to the other – or at random, if there are more than two children playing. If the other child catches the ball, he then throws it back to the original player – or on to someone new, if there are several children.

If anyone fails to catch the ball, he must suffer a forfeit (see below) and then the throwing continues. Forfeits for dropped balls can be reversed if the player catches the ball on the next go. If he misses again, another forfeit is added on. Finally if a ball is dropped while the child is lying down, he is out. The last person still in the game is the winner.

Forfeits
Penalties for missed catches go in the following order:
* Go down on one knee
* Go down on two knees
* Put one hand behind the back
* Lie down flat on the grass.

Tips for beginners
• Make sure the distance between the children is smaller with younger ones.
• Play the game by throwing the ball round in a circle rather than at random.

Age range 7+
Number of players Four or more
Energy level 3
What you will need A large foam ball

Spot

In this high-energy ball game, also known as 'spud', players work hard to avoid turning into a 'spot' by collecting the four letters of the name, and try to be the last person left in.

How to play

Play starts with one person holding the ball and the others surrounding her. She then shouts out someone's name, throws the ball high up into the air and runs away. The player whose name has been called tries to catch the ball – all the others run away.

If the person whose name has been called catches the ball without it bouncing, he can then call out another player's name in the same way and throws to them.

If he misses, or the ball bounces, he shouts 'Spot!' and everyone must freeze. He then picks a player, takes three steps towards her, and throws the ball to try and hit her body or legs. If he's successful, the person who is hit 'collects' the S of Spot. If he misses, or the person catches the ball, the thrower himself collects the S. Then it's the throwee's turn to throw the ball.

Play continues like this until someone has collected all four letters of 'Spot' – and is out. More players will gradually fall out until the last person left in is the winner.

Variation

Adapt this game for younger children by playing it in a circle, throwing randomly across to each other. If someone drops the ball, he collects the first letter of a three-letter word, such as Cat, Dog or Hen. As soon as he has collected all three letters and the word is complete, he is out.

Tip for beginners

Establish a boundary, beyond which no player is allowed to run.

Web ball

Age range 10+
Number of players Six or more
Energy level 1
What you will need Several small balls

'Web ball' starts out fairly simply, but quickly becomes very tricky – it's great for encouraging concentration and cooperation. The intention is to add as many balls into the game as possible without dropping any of them.

How to play

Ask the children to stand in a circle with a reasonable amount of space between them. Explain that during the game everyone will need to remember two people: the person who throws the ball to them, and the person to whom they throw the ball.

Give the first ball to one child, who calls out the name of the person she is going to throw to and then throws the ball. The child who receives the ball calls out the name of another child and throws the ball on to them, and so on.

When everyone has got used to the ball circulating in the same way each time, a second ball is introduced and play continues, with everyone calling out names, throwing and catching in the same sequence.

Once this is established, a third ball is added, and so on, until a ball is finally dropped. Record the most number of balls used and how long each game takes, to find the best.

Tips for beginners
• Use larger balls.
• Throw them more slowly.
• Throw around the circle rather than across it.

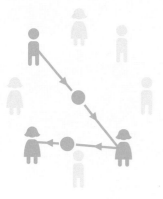

Stage one

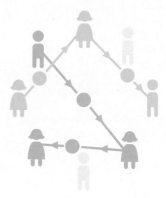

Stage two

Ball against the wall

Age range 9+
Number of players One
Energy level 1
What you will need A bouncy ball, such as a tennis ball; a brick wall without windows

This countdown game is a great way for children to have fun with a ball on their own, by trying to get through all ten of the countdown tasks without dropping the ball. It's challenging, but practice makes perfect!

How to play

Throw the ball against the wall, completing the following challenges:

- 10 sets of throwing the ball, allowing it to bounce once and catching it
- 9 sets of throwing the ball, allowing it to bounce once, clapping once and catching it
- 8 sets of throwing the ball, allowing it to bounce once, clapping twice and catching it
- 7 sets of throwing the ball under the leg, allowing it to bounce once and catching it
- 6 sets of throwing the ball with the best hand, allowing it to bounce once and catching it
- 5 sets of throwing the ball with the worst hand, allowing it to bounce once and catching it
- 4 sets of throwing the ball without any bouncing, and catching it
- 3 sets of throwing the ball, without any bouncing, clapping once and catching it
- 2 sets of throwing the ball, without any bouncing, clapping twice and catching it
- 1 set of throwing the ball, spinning around and catching it.

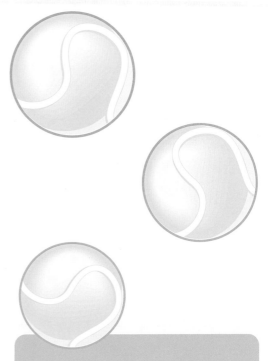

Variations

* You can add new challenges, such as: a third clap; allowing the ball to bounce twice; throwing it under the other leg; bending down to touch the ground; touching both elbows and the nose; and so on.
* Children could try playing this by simply throwing the ball into the air, rather than against a wall – but it will be harder.

Sixty-six

Age range 9+
Number of players Three or more
Energy level 2
What you will need A football; a whistle; a goal (or equivalent)

This football-based game can be played with just a few children – but they do need to work as a team! The aim is to score as many goals as possible before the goalkeeper reaches a count of 66.

How to play

One child is the goalkeeper, the others are the opposing team. When the whistle blows, the goalkeeper begins to count to 66, while the team players pass the ball to each other and try to score goals. The catch is that goals can only be scored with a volley (that is, the ball must be passed by another player and not touch the ground before being shot into goal).

If the team manages to score a goal, the goalkeeper has to revert to counting from one again. But next time around the team will need to score two goals before the goalkeeper goes back to counting from one again. Then it will be three goals, four goals, and so on.

However, if the goalkeeper saves the ball, he swaps places with the player who scored the goal. And once he has managed to count up to 66, he automatically swaps places with the last person to touch the ball.

Tip for beginners

This game works best when players cooperate with each other, so remind the children to work together to score as many goals as they can.

First to 100!

Age range 9+
Number of players Three or more
Energy level 3
What you will need A ball

This is a good game for honing children's adding skills, since they are trying to be the first person to reach 100 points. The arithmetic can be made more challenging for older children (see the variations below).

How to play

The first player throws the ball in the air and calls out a number between 10 and 50 in units of tens (10, 20, 30, 40, 50). If another player catches the ball without it bouncing, he 'collects' that score. If he catches it with one bounce, he collects half the score. If he almost catches it, but subsequently drops it, he deducts the score from any points that he's already collected (he remains at zero if he didn't have any points to begin with). If no one catches the ball, no points are collected.

The player who now has the ball is the next to throw it and calls out a new number. Play continues like this, with each person collecting their scores until one person reaches 100 – and wins the game.

Variations

* Use larger number units (say 25s) and collect points up to 500.
* Alternatively, rather than calling out numbers at random, award fixed points for different types of catching: 20 points for catching the ball without dropping it; 15 points for catching it with one bounce; 10 points for two bounces; and 5 points for claiming it from the ground.

Tip for beginners

For younger children, count only up to 10 and award them one point for every catch they get, regardless of whether or not the ball bounced.

Rounders

Age range 7+
Number of players Minimum of eight (four per team), with two adult helpers
Energy level 2
What you will need Four markers; a bat; a soft ball

This classic playground game works best with a big group of players in an open space. Players strive to score as many rounders as possible during their team's turn at batting, by hitting the ball as far as they can without it being caught.

Tip for beginners

Make sure the adult helper is the bowler. Underarm bowling makes it as easy as possible for the batters to hit the ball.

Preparation

Divide the players into two teams, Team A and Team B, each with an adult helper. Set up a marker to form a stump at each corner of a square playing area.

How to play

Team A bat first. Team B have a fielder guarding each of the four stumps.

Team B's bowler bowls the ball to Team A's first batter. Once she's hit the ball, she drops the bat and runs off towards the first stump. If no one has caught the ball yet, she can continue to the second, third and fourth stumps. If she makes it all the way round, she scores a full rounder. If, however, she sees that the ball has been caught, she waits at whichever stump she's reached. If the

fielders catch the ball and touch the stump before the running batter reaches it, she is caught out. No stump can have more than one player at a time waiting there.

If a batter has hit the ball, but has to wait at the second or third stump for fear of being caught out, she can set off again once the next batter has hit the ball and started to run. If she reaches the fourth stump safely, she scores half a rounder.

The game continues until all the batters have been caught out, when the teams swap sides. The team with the most rounders is the winner.

Variation
For older, faster players, set the stumps further apart to make running between them harder. This gives other players who are fielding a better chance of catching them out between stumps.

Get back!

Age range 7+
Number of players Four or more
Energy level 3
What you will need A landmark to act as 'home'

This chasing game tests all the players' nerves – and speed. It's best played in a big open space with some potential hiding areas. The aim is for players to get back 'home' without being caught.

Preparation
Everyone agrees on which landmark is home – it could be a jumper on the grass, a garden chair or a picnic table.

How to play
All the players gather at home. One player is chosen to be the chaser and counts to at least 20 to give the others a chance to run and hide. Then he calls out 'Ready' and starts to look for the other players. They must emerge from hiding, or sneak into another hiding place nearer home, while the chaser looks for them.

When the chaser sees another player attempting to make it home, he runs to catch her – if he touches her, the other player joins his team and has to chase the hidden players, too.

Eventually all the players will either be back at home or caught and on the chaser's team. Another person is then chosen to be the chaser.

Variations

* The game can start again with the chaser's expanded team all counting to 20 and then trying to catch the remaining players, until everyone has been caught and is on the chaser's team. The last person to be caught becomes the chaser for a new game.
* When a player has been caught by the chaser, she is out (instead of joining the chaser's team). So the winner is the last player who hasn't yet been caught, as long as she gets back to home safely.
* Try adding different characters to the game, such as knights chasing dragons, dogs chasing cats or cats chasing mice.
* If there aren't many good hiding places, the players can simply spread out and try to run back home by dodging the chaser.

Tip for beginners

Give younger players an extra 'life' or two, so that they have a second chance to escape if they're caught too quickly.

Tail end

Age range 6+
Number of players Six or more
Energy level 3
What you will need Enough socks in two different colours for each player to be given a 'tail'

Based on the same principle as 'Tag rugby', which is often played in primary schools, this fun game is a great way for children to burn off energy trying to capture the 'tails' of the opposing team.

Variations

* Handicap stronger or faster players by making their team have fewer members, or by making them walk fast rather than run.
* Use shorter socks to make them a trickier target to grab.
* The referee can be strict about cheating – giving anyone who touches another player 'time out' for a few minutes.
* Players who have captured tails have to tuck them into their own waistband, giving the other team players a chance to win them back.
* Set a time limit to the game. The team with most tails is the winner.

Tip for beginners

Use tights rather than socks to make it easier to catch a tail.

Preparation

The players divide into two teams. Each team chooses a sock colour – for example, grey for Team A, black for Team B. Each team member is given a sock in their team's colour, and has to tuck it into their waistband at the back. Now all the players have a tail.

If playing in an open area, decide where the boundaries of the 'pitch' are and make this clear to all the players.

How to play

The players spread out around the pitch. When you say 'GO!' they run around trying to capture the tails of the opposing team.

They are not allowed to touch or hold other players in any way – they must snatch the tails by skilful running and dodging alone!

Players remain in the game even if they have lost their tail. The winning team is the first to capture all the other team's tails.

Fire and ice

Age range 6+
Number of players Six or more
Energy level 3
What you will need No props

This catching game has a rescue element, too, the aim being to avoid being frozen by the ICE players or melted by the FIRE players, or to rescue other FIRE or ICE players! It's similar to 'Stuck in the mud' (see page 55), but involves two teams and is suited to slightly older players.

How to play

The players divide into two teams. One team is FIRE, the other ICE.

The ICE players have to try and touch the FIRE players as they run around. If an ICE player succeeds in touching a FIRE player, the latter has to freeze straight away in whatever position he's in. He isn't allowed to move again until one of his FIRE team companions touches him to warm him up. Then he unfreezes and can run off again.

The game continues until the ICE players have succeeded in freezing all the FIRE players. Then it is the FIRE team's turn to catch the ICE players, who have to melt into a heap on the ground when they are touched, until they are refrozen by another ICE player.

Variation

If you don't have enough players for two full teams, make the fastest player ICE, while all the others are FIRE.

Tip for beginners

Practise making 'ice statue' shapes before the game, so that the players understand they have to stop running once a member of the ICE team has touched them.

What's the time, Mr Wolf?

Age range 3+
Number of players Two or more
Energy level 2
What you will need No props

This classic childhood game has a scary build-up of tension that's just right for younger players, who will love trying to escape from the clutches of big, bad, hungry Mr Wolf.

Variation

The wolf can pretend to be asleep as the children creep up on him. When they're almost there, he wakes up with a start and chases them all back to the starting line.

Tip for beginners

For very young players, it's best if the wolf allows them all to escape back to the starting line. He can then huff and puff crossly about still being hungry, and begin the game again.

How to play

The children line up together at a distance from the 'wolf' – usually the adult – who has his back to them. The children then call out together, *'What's the time, Mr Wolf?'*

The wolf turns round slowly and replies, *'Two o'clock.'*
The children then take two steps towards the wolf, and ask again, *'What's the time, Mr Wolf?'*

They take steps nearer to him each go, depending on what time Mr Wolf says it is. Once they are almost on a level with the wolf, they ask again, *'What's the time, Mr Wolf?'*

He turns round and roars, *'Dinner time!'* and chases them all back to the starting line.

Whichever child he catches then becomes Mr Wolf for the next game.

Age range 8+
Number of players Four or more
Energy level I
What you will need A tennis ball

Pat ball

Another playground favourite, this game adapts well to the garden or any playing area where there's a wall. Players must attempt to keep the ball bouncing against the wall for as long as possible, using only their hands as rackets.

How to play

The players stand in a row next to each other, a few feet away from the wall. The first player bounces the ball on the ground, then 'pats' it with her hand to make it bounce against the wall. The next player has to let it bounce, then 'pat' it again so that it hits the wall. Play continues along the team, until one of the players either:

• Fails to hit the ball, or
• Hits the ball on the volley, instead of letting it bounce first.

If this happens, the player is out.

If the ball bounces and is hit, but strikes the bottom of the wall where it meets the ground, this is known as 'mids'. Like a 'let' in tennis, that player is allowed another turn.

The player who keeps going longest without dropping the ball is the winner.

Variation
Try using a small bouncy rubber ball for a real challenge.

Tips for beginners
• Use a bigger ball.
• Allow more bounces between players to keep the game going.

Red Rover

Age range 9+
Number of players Ten or more
Energy level 2
What you will need No props

This very robust game is best kept for older players who don't mind some rough and tumble – in fact, they'll probably love it! The plan is to break through the other team's defences and capture their players.

How to play

The players divide into two teams. Each team lines up on either side of the playing area and links arms.

One team then gathers in a 'huddle' and secretly decides which player they will pick from the other team. If they've chosen a boy called Peter, they would then line up, linking arms, and call out:

Red Rover, Red Rover,
Send PETER right over.

Peter then has to run from the other side and try to break through the team's linked arms. If he breaks through successfully, he returns to his own team, taking a player of his choice back with him. If he can't break through, he has to join the opposite team.

Then it's the other team's turn to pick a player to try to break through the opposing defences. The winning team is the one with the most players once everyone's name has been called.

Variation

To make a break-through easier, the team can hold hands instead of linking arms.

Tip for beginners

Make sure there's plenty of room behind each team, as it may take a while for the Red Rover to come to a standstill once he's broken through the line!

Age range 6+
Number of players Minimum of four
Energy level 3
What you will need A baton or ball for
team members to pass

Relay race

This game is great for kids who don't like
being chased, but enjoy the excitement
of competitive running and team spirit.
They're attempting to be part of the first
team to complete the race.

How to play
Divide the players into teams and establish the
boundaries of the race clearly.

Both teams start from the same place. The first
runner is given a ball or baton. On the command
'Go!' she runs as fast as possible to a given point
at some distance – for example, a tree. She has to
touch it with the ball, then run back to the start,
where she hands the ball on to the next player,
who runs off to the tree again.

The relay race continues until all the players on
each team have run the course and one team has
got back to the start first.

Variation
Handicap faster players by making them run
round the tree, or bounce the ball off it
three times before being allowed to set off
back to the starting line.

Tip for beginners
You can plan the race around a circuit,
where players start from a set position
around the course. They have to take the
ball or baton from the previous player as
she runs up to them.

The next three games are all classics that used to be played on school sports days, but work very well as team games for groups of children.

Three-legged race

Age range 5+
Number of players Four or more, but there must be even numbers to pair up
Energy level 2
What you will need Scarves or strips of soft cloth to tie the legs together

The three-legged race looks much more straightforward than it actually is, and demands good coordination with a partner to avoid tumbles. The aim is for the three-legged partnership to get to the finishing line first – without either (or probably both) of them falling over.

Preparation

Each player finds a partner, and they then stand together side by side while you tie their inside legs together with a scarf or strip of cloth at ankle level – so that, in effect, each pair of players has three legs.

How to play

Each pair lines up at the starting line. When you call out 'Go!' they set off, trying to walk or run together by moving their joined-together legs forward, followed by their own 'free' legs in unison. The winning pair is the couple who reach the finish line first.

Tips for beginners
• Match players who are roughly the same size and weight, so that it's easier for them to coordinate their steps.
• If the players put their arms around each other's waists, it's much easier to balance.

Variation
Try playing individually by tying each player's ankles together so that they have to hop to the finish line as fast as possible without falling over.

Hot rocks

Age range 5+
Number of players Three or more
Energy level 1
What you will need Several dessertspoons or tablespoons; the same number of large pebbles or small potatoes

In this 'Egg and spoon' standby of school sports days – where players try to be the first over the finishing line without dropping their 'egg' from its spoon – it's much easier and less wasteful to use pebbles instead of the real thing!

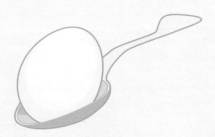

How to play

Each player is given a spoon, plus a pebble or potato to balance on it.

The players line up behind the starting line, all holding their spoons and 'rocks' carefully in front of them. On the word 'Go!' they all set off as speedily as possible towards the finish line.

If anyone drops their rock, they must go back to the beginning and start again.

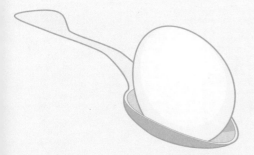

Variation

The classic version of this game is 'Egg and spoon', using hard-boiled eggs instead of potatoes, with players eating their eggs at the end of the race.

Tip for beginners

Younger players can be allowed to put their pebble back on the spoon, instead of having to go back to the beginning.

Wheelbarrow race

Age range 6+
Number of players At least four
Energy level 3
What you will need No props

This is a game for strong arms and straight legs, otherwise the partnership will end up in a tangled heap as it attempts to be the first 'wheelbarrow' to cross the finishing line.

Preparation
Each player chooses a partner. One player lies on the ground and puts his arms out straight, while the other holds his legs by the ankles, to form a 'wheelbarrow'.

How to play
On the word 'Go!' the wheelbarrows set off towards the finish line. If any of the wheelbarrows collapses – either arms or legs – they are out, or have to start again. The winning wheelbarrow is the one that crosses the line first.

Tips for beginners
• Allow younger players to continue even if they collapse on the way to the finish, instead of going back to the beginning.
• Try to ensure that wheelbarrow partners are evenly matched in terms of strength and body weight.

Variations
∗ Three players can form a wheelbarrow, if two players hold one leg each. This is helpful if the player lying down is much heavier than the others.
∗ The wheelbarrow player can wear gloves if the ground is hard.

Grandma's footsteps

Age range 3+
Number of players Four or more
Energy level I
What you will need No props

This game is very easy to play, yet has an element of tension that's just right for younger players, as they make a bid to creep up on Grandma without her spotting any movement.

How to play

One child (or the adult helper) is Grandma and stands with her back to the children, who all line up some distance away.

Whilst Grandma's back is turned, the children creep up slowly towards her. Every now and again she 'wakes up' and turns round suddenly. When she does, all the children must stand as still as statues. If Grandma sees anyone wobbling or moving, they must go back to the beginning.

She then turns back and the players start to creep towards her again. The game continues like this as the children creep ever closer to her. The first person to touch Grandma's back, without her spotting them moving, is the winner.

Variation

Handicap players by making them jump or hop instead of walking up to Grandma. This makes it much harder to keep still when she looks round!

Tip for beginners

Give younger players a second chance if Grandma sees them wobbling, so they can stay in the game longer.

Age range 7+
Number of players Six or more
Energy level 3
What you will need Paper and pencil for writing down the letters (optional)

Red letter day

This lively game encourages spelling skills, as well as expending lots of children's energy. They have to guess the other team's word by catching each player and finding out what their letters are.

Preparation
The players divide into two teams. Each team chooses a word made up of the same number of letters as there are children in the team. For example, if there are three children in each team, both teams secretly choose a three-letter word, such as FOX or CAT.

Four-letter words could be LEAF or TWIG.

Five-letter words could be GRASS or RIVER. And so on.

Each child in the team is assigned one of the letters that makes up the whole word.

How to play
The first team are given a few seconds to run away, before the second team chases after them. If they catch anyone, the player who is caught has to reveal his letter. The second team carry on catching the other team's players until they've discovered enough letters to guess the word.

Then the teams swap roles, and the first team try to discover the other team's word.

Variations
* The word has to be a certain subject, such as animals or types of food.
* In small teams, each player can have more than one letter, so that longer words can be used.
* The guessing team are only allowed to guess one word per letter found.

Tip for beginners
Each player can carry the letter written on a small piece of paper in his hand, so that it doesn't get forgotten.

Where's the treasure?

Age range 5+
Number of players One or more
Energy level I
What you will need Some 'treasure' (a few coins will do, especially if they come to about the cost of an ice-cream); a plastic bag

Can a child find the hidden treasure in the sand? If she can, she can keep it! This game, which is reminiscent of tales of pirates and hidden treasure troves, will delight children and is particularly appropriate for the beach, where the 'treasure' can be hidden easily.

Preparation

Put the treasure inside a plastic bag and seal it tightly. Then tell the child to turn her back and cover her eyes – no peeping – while you bury it, quite deeply, in the sand. Mark the spot with a particular stone that you would recognize, so that you know where to find it again; but disguise it by placing other stones around it.

How to play

Draw a large circle in the sand around the spot, then tell the child that the treasure is buried within that circle. It's her job to find it!

Variations

* Give some clues to help locate the treasure, such as: start at the entrance to the cave; face the sea and take three big steps forwards; turn right towards the large rock; go behind the rock and start digging!
* Describe the route in paces, such as: ten paces left, turn right and take five paces; turn left and take three paces; and so on.

Tips for beginners

• Adjust the size of the searching circle according to the age of the children playing – smaller for younger ones, larger for older children.
• Play 'Where are my feet?' instead. Just get your little one to bury your feet in sand and then pretend not to know where they are – they'll find it endlessly amusing.

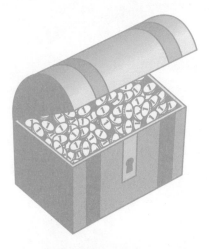

Age range 3+
Number of players At least five, but as many as you like
Energy level 2
What you will need A plastic cricket bat; a tennis ball; something for wickets (sticks, a coolbox or some other item that is to hand)

Beach cricket

All ages can take part in this laid-back game, where the rules are open to debate each time you play! There are no teams (unless you want there to be), and you need only score individual runs if you choose to – the point is to have fun.

Preparation

Find an area of flat sand fairly near the shoreline and as far away from other people as you can. Mark out two 'wickets' (targets that the players have to hit, to get the batters out) a little way apart (say, ten paces) and choose two batters to stand by them.

Tips for beginners
• Don't place the wickets too far apart.
• Instead of a cricket bat, use plastic tennis/badminton rackets and a large soft ball.
• Invent your own rules to suit – the only essential rule is to try and hit the ball and run hard!

How to play

Someone is chosen as a bowler and all the others become fielders (catchers), spacing themselves around the playing area. The bowler throws the ball to the batter, who tries to hit it.

If the batter doesn't hit the first ball, he remains in (getting a second go – and maybe more for younger children). If he misses subsequent balls, he is out.

If he does hit the ball, both batters lay down their bats on the ground and run back and forth between the wickets as many times as they can.

A fielder may get a batter out by catching the ball, by picking it up and throwing it to hit the wicket, or by rolling the ball to hit the bat lying on the ground. If the fielder gets a batter out, he then becomes the new batter.

If the ball goes into the sea/rockpool/cave/sand dune/picnic blanket, the batter automatically scores six runs and is out.

Castle magic

Age range 5+
Number of players Two or more
Energy level 2
What you will need A bucket and spade for each child; lots of shells and pebbles; packs of sandcastle flags (or other suitable items) for prizes

A flat expanse of untouched sand just cries out for a sandcastle competition. In this game each team tries to make a beautiful, individual sandcastle within an agreed time limit; the results are then judged to decide the best one.

How to play

If there are more than two children, divide them into two teams. Mark out an area of sand where each team is to build their sandcastle. Then tell them they have an hour (half an hour for younger children) to each build a sandcastle as *different* from the other team as they can. Build

excitement by calling out how much time they
have left at certain intervals: half an hour, ten
minutes, five minutes, one minute.

At the end of the hour, judge their efforts – and
award prizes! Of course all the castles get praised
for their own specialities and all the teams get a
prize: sandcastle flags with which to decorate
their creation.

Tips for beginners

• Pair a child with an adult. Get a third adult
  to judge.
• Make the time limit flexible, and end the
  game when you feel the child is losing
  interest or getting tired.

Tricks of the trade

To help them get started, you could ask the
following questions:
* Do they want a round or a square castle?
* Do they want a moat? Or two moats
  surrounding the castle?
* How about a drawbridge? Large, flat
  pebbles usually work well for this.
* Would they like a symmetrical or
  asymmetrical castle?
* Do they want corner towers?
* Could they make towers of different sizes?
  They could use buckets, picnic cups,
  disposable drinks cups, yogurt/fromage-
  frais pots or other containers.
* Would a spiral path up to the top be a
  good idea?
* What will they use for decoration? Perhaps
  shells, small pebbles, twigs or seaweed.
* Have they tried the dribbling technique
  (where very wet sand is dribbled into
  mini-mounds)?
* Who lives in their castle: soldiers, kings
  and queens, wizards, witches, fairies, and
  so on?

All my own work

Age range 3+
Number of players One or more
Energy level 2
What you will need A bucket and spade; bits of decoration

If children don't fancy making a sandcastle, get them to make a sand sculpture instead. This allows their creativity to come to the fore as they build an artwork out of sand – and the finished result is open to interpretation!

How to play

There are no rules for this activity, which stems from the child's imagination, but here are some ideas to try:

• **Boat/car**
Dig an oval hole, using the excess sand to build up the front, back and sides. Then make a bench seat of sand, use a paper plate as a steering wheel and press in some shells or pebbles for buttons and controls.

• **Rocket**
Use a similar design to the boat, but make the front end more pointed to form a nose.

• **Mermaid**
Build up a curved pile of sand that tapers into a tail. Add arms, mark out scales on the lower half of the body and draw facial features at the top. Use seaweed for hair.

• **Dog**
Make an oval body of raised sand, then add a head, four legs and a tail. Mark the eyes with pebbles and outline the ears with shells.

• **Cat**
Make a large round body, then add a small round head and a long tail. Finish with two sticking-up ears, some eyes and plenty of seaweed whiskers.

• **Sandman**
Draw round the child in the sand, then build up a raised body shape. Mark out features and clothes with a stick.

• **Face**
Mark out a big circle in the sand and 'draw' in features with different-sized shells. Add flowing seaweed hair.

• **Name**
Build 3D letters of the child's name, mark the letters out in pebbles or simply write them with a stick in wet sand.

Age range 5+
Number of players Two or more
Energy level 1
What you will need A flat area of wet sand; a stick; some small pebbles

Tot it up

This throw-and-count target game is a bit like Tiddlywinks, only on a larger scale and played on the beach. The aim is to score as many points as possible by throwing pebbles onto numbered circles in the sand.

Tip for beginners
Play in pairs, matching up younger children with older ones.

Preparation
Draw five concentric circles in the wet sand with a stick. Write the number 5 in the smallest middle circle, 4 in the next one, 3 in the next one, 2 in the next one and 1 in the last and largest circle.

How to play
Give each child three small pebbles and get them to stand behind a starting line in the sand. Then tell them to take turns to throw their pebbles into the circles to score as many points as they can. If a pebble lands on a line, the lower of the two numbers is taken. The person with the most points at the end of three rounds is the winner.

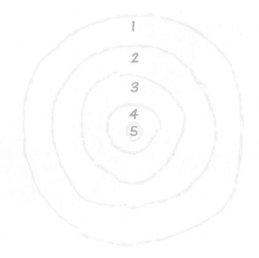

Variations
* Up the challenge by marking each circle with higher scores, such as 50, 25, 15, 10, 5.
* Mark different starting lines for different ages of players.

Castle destroyer

Age range 5+
Number of players Two or more
Energy level I
What you will need A bucket and spade; a small soft ball

This is similar to the classic bowling-alley game of Skittles, but has five sandcastle targets to aim at rather than skittles. Players have to knock down as many castles as they can.

Preparation

Using the bucket, make six sandcastles, laying them out in one row of three, with one row of two behind and then a row of one. Alternatively, simply lay them out in a long row. Draw lines in the sand down each side of the run-up, to make a bowling 'alley'.

How to play

Players take turns to throw the ball and try to knock the sandcastles down. Each person can have three goes at throwing in their turn. Then the castles are built up again for the next player. The winner is the one with the most hits after three rounds.

Age range 4+
Number of players One or more
Energy level 1
What you will need A bucket for each child

Shell hunt

Collecting shells is always a favourite beach pastime – and there are lots of things you can do with them later at home. Children love finding and classifying shells, and seeing who can find the largest/smallest/prettiest ones.

How to play
Give each child a bucket and ask them to collect as many shells in it as they can before you call 'Time's up!'.

When they come back, ask them to sort their shells into rows of similar types: mussel shells, cockle shells, spiral shells, limpet shells, scallop shells, and so on. Identify them with a shell book, if you have one. Shells that have both halves are especially good. Then help the children count them and see how many they have of each type – you could even make a chart, if you wish.

Supershells
Don't know what to do with your shells when you've got them home? Here are some ideas:
• Press shells into playdough to make seaside patterns.
• Make a display by laying the most complete shells on cotton wool in a box with cardboard dividers.
• Paint the back of scallop shells in rainbow colours, like a giant fan. Finish off with a layer of varnish.
• Buy a plain wood-frame mirror and stick the shells all around the outside to decorate it.
• Stick the shells onto a box (round cheese boxes are ideal) to keep jewellery in.
• Using stiff card as a base, experiment with making a variety of shell people and animals, gluing them together when you're happy with the result.

Variations
* If you're on a pebble beach, collect pebbles and stones instead of shells, looking out for interesting colours, shapes and oddities, such as sea-polished glass.
* Try building a tower of pebbles and have a competition to see who can build the highest tower without it collapsing.
* Skim flat stones across the sea and see how many times they bounce. Always check for swimmers first, though!
* Put a large stone down as a target and let each child take turns at throwing smaller stones to hit it – each child can have three throws in a turn. The one with the most hits is the winner. (Warn players and bystanders to stand well out of the way while the throwing is going on.)

Boat races

Age range 7+
Number of players Two or more
Energy level 1
What you will need Bits and pieces to improvise a boat (see the suggestions below)

Get children to use their ingenuity to make improvised boats, then build their own watercourse, so that they can race their boats down a rivulet and see who gets to the finish first.

Preparation

First get the children to make their boats. These can be anything from a raft made of twigs to a more fancy creation made from cut-down plastic bottles, with a mast made from a plastic straw and a sail from a paper bag. They can make it any way they like – the only essential is that it floats.

How to play

Now find a fairly wet bit of sand with some shallow pools, or get them to dig a mini-trench to act as the 'river'. Children will probably have lots of fun building dams in various places to direct the water flow. Then, placing the boats in the water at the same time, let the race begin!

Tip

If children are using man-made items to make their boats, make sure that you collect all the bits at the end, to avoid causing environmental damage.

Variation

A timeless game that can be played wherever there's water flowing under a bridge is to follow the progress of a favourite stick from one side of a bridge to the other, just as Winnie-the-Pooh and friends did in the game of Poohsticks.

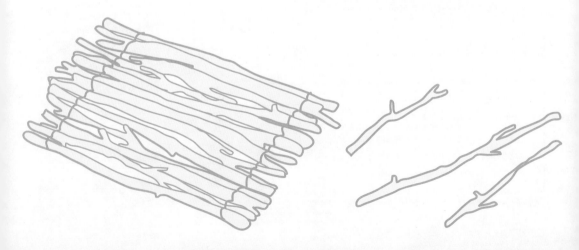

Age range 4+
Number of players One or more
Energy level 2
What you will need A paper bag; a hole
punch; ring reinforcements; wool; tissue
paper; glue

Up, up and away!

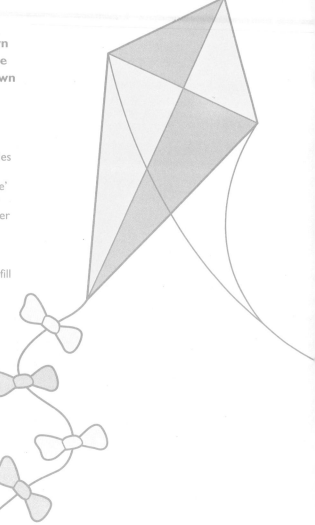

Help a child make his own kite and fly
it along the beach. There's something
very exhilarating about seeing your own
creation dip and weave like a bird in the
air, and the satisfaction of flying your own
kite is immense.

Preparation
Open the paper bag slightly and punch two holes
on each side. Strengthen them with paper ring
reinforcements. Then, on each side, tie a 'handle'
of wool and join the two handles with another
long length of wool. Glue some thin tissue-paper
streamers to the bottom of the bag.

How to play
Now open out the bag fully and run! It should fill
with wind and fly.

Hit the hole

Age range 7+
Number of players Two or more
Energy level 1
What you will need Plastic golf clubs (or other bats); small soft balls; a spade

This is a golf-type game that is played in a circle instead of a straight line. Players are trying to be the first person to get right round the circuit and back to the beginning again.

Preparation
First, dig a hole in the sand a little larger than the size of the largest ball. Then draw a very big circle around the hole (as big as you can make it in the space available) and mark several points off along the circumference (at least one pace apart).

How to play
Starting at the top of the circle, players take turns to hit their balls into the hole. Once a ball is in, the player can collect it and move on to the next point in the circle. The first person to get back to the beginning is the winner.

Variation
Create a crazy golf course around the circuit making 'bunkers', mounds and channels in the sand that players have to negotiate on their way to the hole.

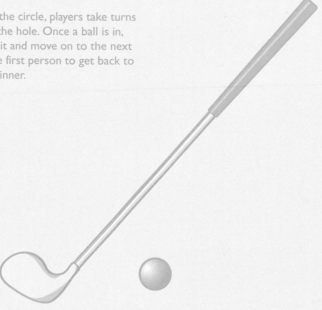

Age range 3+
Number of players One or more; *and make sure there is an adult in attendance*
Energy levels 1–3
What you will need No props, except perhaps a beach ball or body board

In the swim

Paddling and swimming In the sea are a real treat and a great form of exercise, but need to be approached with caution because of tides and currents. However, with adult supervision, children can have tremendous fun in the shallows.

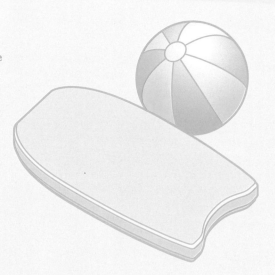

How to play
Here are some ways for children to enjoy the water safely:

• Very young children will enjoy playing 'wave chase', where they stand at the water's edge, holding your hand and running away from an incoming wave onto the beach. They've 'won' if the wave doesn't touch their feet – but 'losing' is probably more exciting!
• Slightly older children will enjoy 'leapsies' – a paddling game where they have to leap over an incoming wave.
• Beginner swimmers will enjoy being in the water with you and 'swimming', parallel to the shore, with you standing in front and holding their hands to guide them along.
• Older children who are confident swimmers can play swimming races, or 'Piggy in the middle' (see page 70) with a beach ball. But they *must* know how to stay safe in the water (see Sea safety, right).
• Teenagers will probably love using a body board or surfboard.

Sea safety
* Read all beach safety notices.
* Children must only swim between the safe range of the flags.
* They should always swim parallel to the shore, not out to sea.
* Make sure children stay within their depth.
* They must always have an adult nearby in the water with them.

On the rocks

Age range 5+
Number of players One or more; *and make sure there is an adult in attendance*
Energy level 1
What you will need A fishing net; a bucket; jelly shoes

Who hasn't got fond memories of exploring rockpools on the beach – unless of course you slipped and fell in! In these activities children explore what interesting natural discoveries they can make in rockpools.

How to play

To make a rockpool exploration more of a game, ask the child if she can fish in the water with her net and find five different things to put in her bucket (with a little water). These might include: a shrimp, some floating bits of seaweed, a pebble, an empty mussel shell, a pretty periwinkle shell or an unoccupied crab shell.

Then ask her to show you five other things that she can't pick up, such as a limpet, a barnacle, some rooted seaweed, a mussel colony, a starfish, a living crab or an anemone.

Tips for beginners

• Choose rocks that are easy to climb over, with flat, dry, unslippery surfaces.
• Make sure there is no danger of being cut off by the tide.
• Always keep water safety in mind – children can drown in only a few inches of water.
• Deeper rockpools are likely to contain a greater selection of creatures and plants than shallower ones.

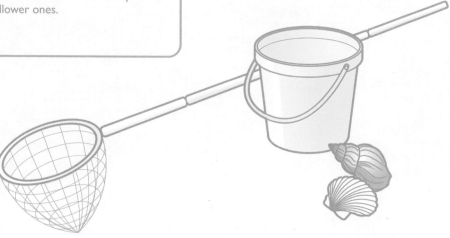

Big fish, little fish

Age range 4+
Number of players Four or more
Energy level 3
What you will need No props

This is a great game to play on the beach if the weather isn't too hot. As it involves running around, you will need a fair bit of clear space in which to play. The purpose is for the Big Fish to catch the Little Fish within a set time limit.

Preparation

With a stick or stone, draw two largish circles in the sand, one inside the other.

How to play

Select one player to be the Big Fish, and ask everyone else to stand with him inside the inner circle. Then choose another player to be the Little Fish, and ask him to stand alone on the sand in the outer circle.

The Big Fish now has to try to escape from the inner circle – while the other players do their best to stop him – and catch the Little Fish, who can only run within the boundary of the outer circle (that is, he can't cross into the inner circle or go outside the outer circle). A time limit is set and the game begins.

If the Big Fish catches the Little Fish within the time limit, the Little Fish becomes the Big Fish and a new Little Fish is chosen. If the Big Fish fails to catch the Little Fish within the time limit, he is out of the game altogether. The Little Fish then becomes the Big Fish, and a new Little Fish is chosen, as before.

Down in the den

Age range 3+
Number of players One or two
Energy level 1
What you will need Sticks/washing line/large cardboard box; old sheets or blankets and cushions; something to act as a table; other items for decorating

Children enjoy the whole process of making a den, from building it to furnishing it and playing in it. If you are in the garden you will have some man-made objects to hand; if not, make the most of any natural objects that you find lying around.

How to play

There are any number of ways to improvise a den, or secret hideout. Here are some ideas to get you started:

• **Wigwam**
Tie some long sticks together at the top, spread them out at the bottom and rest a blanket over them, leaving an open entrance.

• **Cave**
Drape an old blanket or sheet over some low-hanging branches of a tree or bush so that there is a dark interior.

• **Tent**
Hang a large sheet over a washing line and weigh it down with stones.

• **House**
Cut holes in a large cardboard box for windows and doors (old washing-machine and fridge boxes are ideal for this).

Tips for beginners
• Keep it simple – a child's imagination will supply what you can't.
• Make sure there is plenty of ventilation, as the den will quickly get hot inside.

Variations
* For an instant beach den, put two beach chairs back-to-back and drape a large towel over them. Then make a Neptune's cave by gathering several small stones and rocks to make a 'throne' (use a folded beach towel as a cushion, if necessary). Next, decorate the den with seaweed and shells. A child could even cut out some paper fish and hang them on strings pinned to the towel 'ceiling' to finish the effect.
* Instead of making a large den for humans, why not make a miniature one for imaginary fairies/elves? It could have twig walls and roof, a moss floor, a bark table, acorn cups and leaf plates.

To theme your den, here are some ideas for decorating it as a particular place:

• **A cosy home**
Use cherry blossom or an old rug for a carpet, a cushion for a sofa, a large flat stone for a table and some picnic bits and bobs for a make-believe tea.

• **Ice-cream stall**
Put a table in front of the den and make paper ice-creams and lollies to display and sell, with paper money to pay for them.

• **Rescue station**
Use a table as a reception desk, make a cardboard mobile phone and add a pad of paper to record 'disasters'. A rug or towel laid out flat and a pillow can form a 'stretcher'.

Can you find it?

Age range 3+
Number of players One or more
Energy level 1
What you will need Some postcards, a tourist pamphlet, a local information booklet, an 'I spy' book, or simply a list of items you have devised yourself

Young children love 'spotting' games, and discovering new things is a great way to increase their general knowledge and aid their language development. In this game they have to spot as many things in the pictures or list as they can.

Preparation

Collect together some pictures from any of the sources given in 'What you will need' or, for children who can read easily, make a list.

How to play

Give the pictures or list to the child and explain that you are both going on a 'finding adventure' to see if you can find the actual objects. Score a point for every item you discover. Any of the objects in the lists given right and opposite might be good ones to look for – check first that they are definitely available in your location.

On a walk

Depending on the time of year, your list could include the following:

- Acorns
- Conkers
- Pine cones
- Sycamore 'wings'
- Feathers
- Empty egg shells
- Wild flowers (don't pick these)
- Different-shaped or different-coloured leaves
- Trees that are tall and thin, or wide and bushy
- Trees that have bare branches or leafy branches
- Trees with interesting barks (try doing a bark rubbing by placing a piece of paper over the bark and rubbing it with a crayon).

Note Don't touch any mushrooms or berries unless you are sure what they are, and always wash your hands after handling natural objects.

Tips for beginners

- Limit your pictures to about five objects, adding more only if you feel that the child is really enjoying the challenge.
- Always stay with children under eight, and make sure children over eight search in pairs and have clear boundaries – ensuring that they can always see a parent or adult helper is a practical one.
- If a child has a digital camera or a camera phone, he could take pictures of the items to prove his 'finds'.

Variations

You can play this game almost anywhere, including at a theme park, stately home, art gallery or museum. Here are two more 'spotting' lists for the town and seaside.

In the town

A city or town is packed with things to spot, both large and small. Try these:

* Church
* Town hall
* Museum
* Art gallery
* Fountain
* Statue or monument
* Large department store
* Smaller shops
* Office blocks
* Different types of houses and flats
* Chimneys
* TV aerials and dishes
* Interesting brickwork patterns
* Building decorations
* Unusual windows (plate-glass shop windows, Victorian sash windows, stained-glass windows, round windows, skylights, and so on)
* Doors and doorways
* Alleys
* Gateways
* Manhole covers and drains
* Postboxes.

At the seaside

It's not just sea and sand by the coast. Try looking for these things:

* Boats (large/small; with/without sails)
* Flags (safety/sandcastle)
* Stripy deckchair
* Lobster pots
* Bucket and spade
* Lighthouse
* Pier
* Ice-cream kiosk
* Driftwood
* Sea-cleaned glass
* Seagull
* Tea hut
* Shore defences
* Sandcastle
* Sand dune
* Cliff
* Cave
* Seaweed (both brown and green)
* Shells (see also 'Shell hunt', page 105)
* Swimmers
* Surfers
* Lifeguard
* Beach hut.

Pond dipping

Age range 3+
Number of players One or more; *and make sure there is an adult in attendance*
Energy level 1
What you will need A pond or shallow pool of still water; a medium-sized shallow dish; a small net

Pond dipping offers a fascinating glimpse of the teeming life that flourishes wherever there is still water, plus a chance to discover the amazing creatures that live so close to us, but which we so often fail to notice.

How to play

Dip the shallow dish into the pond so that there's a little water in it. Then skim the net just under the surface of the pond. Carefully tip the net inside out into the water in the dish. Put the dish down carefully on the ground and inspect it to find out which creatures you've caught. When you've finished, carefully slip the water from the dish back into the pond, releasing the creatures into their natural environment.

Variations

* Children can take a pad and paper along too, and sketch some of the insects and pond creatures that they find. When they get home, they can do some research to find out what they're called.
* At the beach, rockpools offer a variety of different creatures (see page 110).
* Get children to notice how the different pond creatures swim, and see if they can imitate them – on dry land, of course!

Tip for beginners

An adult will need to supervise the net-dipping to ensure the bottom of the pond is not disturbed.

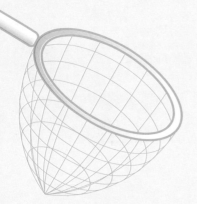

Age range 4+
Number of players One or more
Energy level 2
What you will need A carrier bag for each
player for their finds

Picture this

This game encourages children to use
their imagination to seek out a selection
of natural objects, which can then be
used to make a display or picture after
the walk, preserving them as a keepsake.

How to play

Set off for a nature walk, choosing open parkland,
woodland, seaside or whatever is close by. Each
person searches for interesting objects that can
be carried easily. These might include leaves,
flowers, grasses, blossom, seeds or seedpods,
and so on.

Players collect the objects carefully in a bag, then
make a display of them at home or stick them
onto paper or card to make a collage. Always
wash your hands afterwards.

Tip for beginners

Take younger children on a tree hunt –
finding lots of different leaves of trees and
seeing if you can identify them. Get them
to look for at least ten.

Variation

Children can press leaves, grasses or flower
heads inside the pages of a heavy book, leave
them for a week, then stick them onto paper
for a lasting display. They may want to glaze
the picture or put it behind glass in a frame.

It's categorical

Age range 7+
Number of players One or more
Energy level 1
What you will need Paper and pencils

This is a nature-walk version of the classic pencil-and-paper game of categories. It's also a variation of the spotting game 'Can you find it?' (see page 114), with the objects sorted into groups this time.

Preparation

Each player draws a row of columns on their paper. At the top of each column they write the name of a different category, such as:

• Animal
• Bird
• Flower
• Tree

How to play

As you walk through the park or woods, each player has to write down at least five of each category that they have seen. The winner is the first to complete their sheet.

Variations

* For older players, make the categories more specific, such as the names of trees: pine, oak, maple, beech, yew, and so on.
* Or try the classic *animal, vegetable, mineral*, with ten things to find in each category.

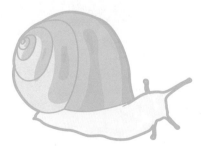

Tip for beginners

For younger players, take away the competitive element of the game and simply enjoy finding one of each category.

What am I like?

Age range 5+
Number of players One or more
Energy level 1
What you will need No props

This game is great for youngsters, who can have fun identifying the characteristics of the things seen on walks and discovering exactly what makes each creature or thing the way it is.

How to play

Go for a walk outdoors – it doesn't have to be in a wide open space; an urban area works just as well. The first player (usually the adult) spots something, such as a bird or squirrel, and asks if the other player can identify its characteristics.

For example, if it's a bird, the questions for a young player might be:

• Can it *swim* or does it *fly*?
• Does it have *fur* or *feathers*?
• Do its babies come from *eggs*?
• Does it live in a *nest* or in a *burrow*?

Tips for beginners
• Keep the questions very simple, such as: 'Is it alive?'
• Young players will enjoy acting out the thing they've identified, such as a bird flying or a tree swaying in the wind.

Variation
Turn the game into a '20 questions' format, where the first player decides on a thing or object, and the other player has to guess what it is by asking 20 questions about it, which can only be answered 'Yes' or 'No'.

Secret trails

Age range 4+
Number of players Two or more
Energy level 2
What you will need A selection of twigs and pebbles; small prizes

The aim of this game is to follow the trail left by secret symbols to the end of the route, where a small prize is hidden. It is best played in a woodland or park with lots of shrubs and pathways.

Preparation
Collect a group of twigs and pebbles, ideally all of a similar shape and colour. The players all need to know what the clues will look like: for example, the twigs will be arranged in arrows, while the pebbles will be set out in a row of three.

How to play
The players hide their eyes while you lay a trail of twig arrows and pebble rows, which they must spot. Each clue leads them in a new direction, until finally they reach the last stage of the trail, where a small prize is hidden for each person or team to find.

Variation
If you know the playing area well – for example, if it's your local park – plan ahead by preparing some written clues that can be found along the way, to make the game into more of a treasure hunt.

Tip for beginners
Keep the trail clues close to each other so that they're easy to spot.

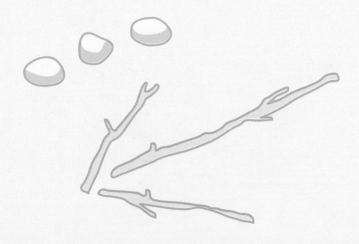

Age range 4+
Number of players One or more
Energy level 2
What you will need Paper and pencils;
clear plastic jar (optional)

Insect hunt

Encourage an interest in the tiniest and
busiest creatures in the open with this
game, which has the players exploring far
and wide to spot and record as many
different insects as possible within a set
time limit.

Preparation

All the players write the names of several
different insects along the top of a sheet of paper.
These might include:

• Ant
• Bee
• Woodlouse
• Fly
• Beetle
• Ladybird
• Butterfly

Younger players can familiarize themselves by
doing the actions for each one – for example,
fluttering like a butterfly or buzzing like a bee.

How to play

Players have ten minutes to search the local
habitat for the insects. Each time they see one,
they can put a tick on their paper in the column
under the insect's name.

The winner is the player who has recorded the
most finds once the time is up.

Variations

* Put one or two ants or beetles in a clear
  plastic jar so that children can look at
  them closely before releasing them again.
* If players find an ants' nest, or see lots of
  ants, mark the papers with a cross for each
  ten ants seen. Warn the children not to
  touch an anthill.

Tips for beginners

• Limit the number of insects to three
  or four.
• Draw pictures of the insects instead of
  writing the names, so that it's easier for
  younger players to spot them.

Memory teaser

Age range 6+
Number of players One or more
Energy level 1
What you will need A cloth big enough to cover a selection of natural items, such as conkers, nuts, seeds, grasses, pebbles and leaves; paper and pencils (optional)

This outdoor version of the traditional 'Kim's game' stretches the players' naming and memory skills. They're trying to see how many of the natural items they can remember and name once they're covered up.

How to play

Players all go out to hunt for suitable natural items (10–20 are usually plenty), which are then set out on a patch of grass. The children all take a good look at the items and say their names out loud as you point to each one.

Cover the items with a cloth and ask players how many things they can remember. They may like to work in two teams, if there are enough players.

Variation

The players all write down their remembered items, and the winner is the one to remember the most items after a two minute time limit.

Tip for beginners

Three or four items are enough for very young players.

Age range 5+
Number of players One or more
Energy level I
What you will need A drawstring bag or a box with a lid; a selection of natural items with interesting textures

Feely finder

This game relies on touch to help the players identify what natural items are being hidden from them in a bag or box. It encourages children to think about texture, rather than concentrating simply on an object's appearance.

How to play

Put a selection of natural items into the bag or box, and ask each player in turn to put one hand in and feel the items. These might include:

- A smooth nut, such as an acorn
- A nut shell
- A tree seed (for example, the 'parachute' seeds of a sycamore)
- A conker
- A leaf (scented ones could gain extra points, if players can identify the smell – such as lavender or mint).

Players can either say out loud what they think the items are, or write them down. The next player does the same, and the winner is the one who guesses all the items correctly.

Tips for beginners
- If the children have helped to collect the items, they'll have a much better chance of guessing what they are.
- Put the items in the box one by one, to make them easier to identify.

Index by age range

Index

Acknowledgements

Executive Editor Jane McIntosh
Editor Charlotte Macey
Design Manager Tokiko Morishima
Designer Ginny Zeal
Senior Production Controller Martin Croshaw
Illustrator Sudden Impact Media